The Inclusion-Classroom
Problem Solver

The Inclusion-Classroom Problem Solver

Structures and Supports to Serve All Learners

Constance McGrath

HEINEMANN
Portsmouth, NH

Heinemann

A division of Reed Elsevier Inc.

361 Hanover Street

Portsmouth, NH 03801–3912

www.heinemann.com

Offices and agents throughout the world

Library of Congress Cataloging-in-Publication Data

McGrath, Constance.

  The inclusion-classroom problem solver : structures and supports to serve all learners / Constance McGrath.

      p. cm.

  Includes bibliographical references and index.

  ISBN-13: 978-0-325-01270-4

  ISBN-10: 0-325-01270-9

  1. Inclusive education—Handbooks, manuals, etc.   2. Children with disabilities—Education—Handbooks, manuals, etc.   3. Classroom environment—Handbooks, manuals, etc.   I. Title.

LC1200.M355 2007

371.9′046—dc22   2007027321

Editor: Harvey Daniels

Production service: Aaron Downey, Matrix Productions, Inc.

Production coordinator: Sonja S. Chapman

Cover design: Jenny Jensen Greenleaf

Typesetter: House of Equations, Inc.

Manufacturing: Steve Bernier

Printed in the United States of America on acid-free paper

11 10 09 08 07   EB   1 2 3 4 5

To my husband Stephen and my daughters, Stephanie and Julia

Contents

Acknowledgments xi

Part 1

Chapter 1 Beginnings 1

The Good, the Bad, and the Wonderful 3
What's the Secret? 4
Every Year There's More to Do 6
Asking the Right Questions 8
Building a Team 9
How This Book Works 10

Chapter 2 A Guide to Common Disabilities 14

Attention Deficit Disorder (ADD/ADHD) 17
Nonverbal Learning Disabilities 21
Asperger's Autism (High-Functioning Autism) 24
Dyslexia 27
Dysgraphia 30
Arithmetical Learning Disability 33
Tourette's Syndrome 36

Part 2

Chapter 3 The Physical Classroom 38

General Classroom Layout 39
Classroom Routines 41
Common IEP Accommodations 41

Math Accommodations 44

Reading Accommodations 47

Writing Accommodations 50

Multiple Pathways of Intelligence 51

**Chapter 4   Curricular Supports
and Accommodations 54**

An Instructive Fable About Instruction 54

Make a New Plan, Stan 56

The Learning Zone 58

A Curriculum Accessible to All 59

What Most Becomes a Teacher 64

Chapter 5   Classroom Climate 66

Being Yourself 68

Expectations, Tolerance, and Accepting Differences 70

Self-Assessment 72

The Classroom Community 74

Promoting Friendships 76

**Chapter 6   "Behavior Problems": What Our
Students Are Trying to Tell Us 81**

"Why Do You Do the Things You Do?" 82

A Powerful New Lens 86

Supporting Positive Behavior in the Inclusive Classroom 87

Changing Your Spots 88

Moving Toward Support for All 91

Giving Disruptive Behavior a Face 93

The Exception to the Rule 95

Chapter 7   Inclusive Classroom Assessment 98

Embedded Assessments 101

Traditional Assessments 101

About Grading 104

Retaking Tests 105

Part 3

Chapter 8 Communicating and Collaborating with Parents 108

    Fostering Collaboration 109

    Reaching Out to Parents 110

    Reporting Progress 112

Chapter 9 Building Your Special Education Team 115

    Planning Together 117

    Team Dynamics 118

    Play a Leadership Role 119

    Use an Inclusive Lens 120

    Know Where We're Going 121

    Weekly Meetings 122

    Rome Wasn't Built in a Day 123

Bibliography 127

Index 129

Acknowledgments

I would like to express my gratitude and appreciation to Smokey Daniels for the guidance that helped this book take shape and to Alan Huisman for his skillful editing.

This book is a result of having observed outstanding teachers bringing the best of teaching practices to life in ways that include and empower all children. I thank all of the teachers with whom I have worked; each of you has made a contribution to this book, and I am indebted to each of you for all you have taught me. I also want to thank the members of the special education team I work with for all that I have learned from you as well: Erica Pilat, special educator; Alyson Lajeunesse, speech and language pathologist; and Elana Wolkoff, school psychologist.

Great administrators are essential to a school district and building. In appreciation of the culture of Sprague Elementary School, I would like to thank Ellen Cunniff, principal, who built and formed it. A special thank you to Beth Brown, Head of Special Education, for being a valued mentor and guide. Thank you also to Dorsey Yearley, Head of Student Services, for her knowledge and leadership.

As much as this book is about what I have learned from the teachers I have worked with, it is also about what I have learned from children. I am equally indebted to and would like to thank the students for what they have taught me about inclusion and the reasons it is so important.

I would also like to thank Sonja Chapman for overseeing the entire project, and Aaron Downey for carefully coordinating all of the details that went into preparing the book for publication. Thanks so much to Jenny Jensen Greenleaf for your great cover design, to Eric Chalek for crafting the cover copy, and to Lisa Koehler for copyediting the manuscript and providing the final polish.

Finally, I would also like to express my appreciation to my husband for not complaining about the extra work he inherited while I was preoccupied with this book and for being my technical support wizard, available to help me whenever disaster struck. I also want to thank Stephanie and Julia, my daughters, for sharing with me their very enlightening thoughts and perspectives on school, education, teachers, and why kids do the things they do.

Beginnings

I t's a beautiful late summer morning, and you know the date without looking at the calendar. The school year starts next week, and there they are,
the conflicting emotions, right on schedule: the small knot in the pit of
your stomach and the sense of excitement in your heart and mind. As of today,
for you, summer is over. Over the next series of days each of these feelings
will grow as you prepare for a new school year.

It is the day before the students arrive. You understand the importance of
the first days of school and have worked hard getting ready. You check each
item off your list:

- There is a welcome sign on the door.
- The bulletin boards are bright and cheerful. (And you've left at least
  one blank, on which you'll display student work.)
- You have posted some basic classroom procedures and set up a birth-
  day board.
- There is a sign-in sheet to help you keep track of attendance; there is
  a sign-out sheet to help you monitor bathroom visits, and you have
  established procedures for the orderly use of computers and books.
- You have designated boxes for homework and finished class work,
  and you have challenge activities ready for those who finish their
  work early.
- You have designed procedures to start the day smoothly. An easel at
  the door will announce the morning work, which children will begin
  independently after signing in and choosing their lunch entree.

- You have purchased a rain stick; the beautiful sound it makes will be your signal for students to quiet down or focus their attention on you.
- You've included a display area where the day's schedule and any homework assignments will always be posted.
- Paper and supplies are organized and accessible.
- The desks are arranged, with name tags attached.
- You have prepared a welcome speech and get-to-know-you activities.
- You have planned (okay, overplanned) lessons for each subject for the first few days of school.
- You are confident about the curriculum; you have studied it and understand the big ideas as well as the day-to-day lessons.

So why is that knot still in your stomach?

Because tomorrow you will meet your students. They will file into your classroom, you will greet each one, and the year will begin. Although anyone looking at your preparations would say you have done a fine and conscientious job, you worry you haven't done enough. But what more can you do? You take one last look at your room, say a prayer, and hope fate is kind. Then you close the door and go home.

That night you anticipate what is to come. Although you'd like to have a "good class" this year (there's no doubt some classes are easier than others), it seems in recent years they have all been challenging. You know that having one child in the class who constantly struggles to learn or is exceptionally disruptive can mean living with a knot in your stomach all year; at worst, you might consider a career change. While you and your students are starting with a clean slate and unlimited optimism, you also know how easy it is to lose a child, to watch in hopeless frustration as that child disengages.

But maybe it isn't fate or luck or even the kids. Sometimes, when you hear that a child who was difficult for you was also difficult the year before or the year after, you feel a little flood of relief. It wasn't you. Other teachers found him or her difficult as well. But still it nags at you. There must be a key—there are teachers who can teach kids who are difficult and don't seem to be pushed to the limit. It must be a rare and special gift though, because from conversations with other teachers you know, most seem to be more like you. Then again, maybe it's not a gift. Maybe some teachers do have the key.

You think back to last June, about the work that went into putting together the group of children you will meet tomorrow. You are well aware that the group was not formed randomly. You know the process of putting together a class for the following year is serious and time consuming. Administrators and teachers at each grade level put an enormous amount of thought into it. They try to group children who are a good influence on one another and separate children who have not worked well together during the current year. Then they try to balance the classes as much as possible. You know this means every class will probably include some actively engaged learners who would do well in any classroom, and that most of the class will be made up of children who do good to adequate work. A few children in the class will need extra help even though they do not have a diagnosed learning disability, and that each class will include one or several children who have documented support needs spelled out in their IEPs.

You also know that while classes were being formed, the teachers were also being thought about and evaluated—by the parents, who hope their child is lucky enough to get a teacher they've heard through the grapevine is really good, the kind of teacher who empowers children as learners, makes them feel successful, and could even have a positive impact that lasts a lifetime—by the principal, who may decide certain children should be with a certain teacher because of that teacher's proven ability to help that type of child thrive—and by the students' current teachers, who have come to know and care about their charges, who also know and care about their colleagues, and who therefore try to recommend placements that do the most good for both the children and the teachers, hoping to increase the odds that everyone at the next grade level will have a good year.

■ The Good, the Bad, and the Wonderful

Most teachers are good at their job. Children spend the year learning and are prepared to go on to the next grade. Here or there is the teacher who can seemingly work wonders with any child; at the other extreme, there is the occasional teacher who will complain about his or her class all year, whoever the children are. What accounts for these differences? What is it that differentiates the best teachers, the good teachers, and those that year after year grumble about the unteachable children in their classes? Is it possible to go from good to great, or even from overwhelmed to great? Can a brand-new teacher have an aura of greatness from the very start? I believe the answer to the last two questions is yes. Is there a key that only a few teachers hold? I believe there is more than one key, there is a giant ring full of keys, of things we can do to be one of the teachers children remember forever and that parents pray their children get. The kind of teacher who, to paraphrase William Butler Yeats, does not just fill the pail but lights a fire—the teacher who is remembered as being wonderful and possibly even life changing.

Teachers who can enjoy even the most challenging students are those who have developed a positive classroom environment, who love their jobs and their students, and who make it possible for the children in their classes to be successful. They encourage children to view themselves as learners, and they let children discover that hard work brings results by acknowledging and rewarding that hard work, even if the product is not always perfect. They are the teachers who work with children to motivate and skillfully challenge them so that they accomplish more than they believe they can, giving them the confidence to believe they can do it again in the future. This is what people mean when they tell you about a great teacher they had when they were children. It is what parents mean when they tell you about a terrific teacher their child had. Most teachers have done this with some children. Great teachers do it with all (or most) children.

■ What's the Secret?

Of all the keys to being a great teacher, the one that makes the most difference, in school as in life, is the lens through which we view the world. Consider some possibilities. Children are shouting and having a heated discussion. Are they fighting, or are they presenting opinions that are important to them? A boy comes to school in a sullen mood without his homework; would your punitive reaction change if you knew that the night before his parents told him they are filing for divorce? You see a man climb into the window of a house at dusk; is it the homeowner who has forgotten his key or a thief intent on robbing the place? In each case you will react very differently depending on the way you view the situation. As educators, one of the most powerful changes we can make is to change the lens we use to view our role in the classroom.

When a child receiving special education services is placed in the general education classroom, some teachers ask, "What does this child have to do to fit into my class, and how am I going to change this child?" They ask these same questions, relative to different children, and experience the same feelings of frustration and being overwhelmed year after year. But for teachers who understand that they teach in an inclusion classroom, that this is their job and it is not going to change, and that teaching all the children in their class is their responsibility, the question becomes, "How can I structure my classroom to accommodate all the children in it?" As these teachers build a foundation of structures and supports that remains and grows from year to year, this question becomes more and more specific: "How can I fine-tune this particular lesson to make this particular child successful?" Teachers who recognize that there will always be children with diverse learning needs in their class make changes to their classrooms for the long haul. Teachers who are hoping for a general education class in which there is no diversity in learning styles and no students with special learning needs are destined to be disappointed, and they run the risk of becoming more disillusioned and embittered as the years pass. They work hard, but the kids with special needs seem to take up all their time. These teachers exert a great amount of effort, but because they are not planning for the long term, the results often fall short.

In most public schools in the twenty-first century, the "general" education classroom does not exist. Over the past decades the number of children with diverse learning needs has continued to increase. At the same time the federal government has tightened the rules regulating when children with diverse learning needs may be taken out of the classroom for instruction. We are required to educate all children in the "least restrictive environment." That definition has been tightened over the years as well. Current guidelines specify that children must be taught in the general education classroom unless it is not possible to provide the necessary instruction in that setting. What this means is that most children with diverse learning needs are in the general education classroom for most of the day. It is a real change, based on the belief that an inclusive classroom is a microcosm of the world we live in and that being a part of one benefits all children. Today, inclusive classrooms are a fact of life (Schwarz, 2006).

If you look around, though, you will see that teachers who take ownership of all the students in their class and believe they can teach all children if they use the right method or accommodation, seem able to deal with even the seemingly most-challenging students and still have a joyful year. This does not happen without planning and hard work, but as fall unfolds it pays off, and things begin to run smoothly. These teachers enjoy their work and are able to establish an effective collaboration with special educators. They feel they have the support they need and the ability to do their job well. They have a great reputation within the school and with parents. They seem genuinely fond of all the children in their classroom, and the kids like them back. They make teaching look like fun.

These teachers understand that they teach in an inclusive classroom, and to better serve in it they have built in many permanent accommodations. When a child with a specific need comes along, they can add new accommodations that become part of their classroom structure, not just for this child but for the long term. Over time, they have discovered that these accommodations benefit all, including the typical children in the class.

■ Every Year There's More to Do

Over the years the curriculum has changed as well. Teachers are expected to teach a broader curriculum than in years past, and it is expected that the children in the class will do well on state-mandated exams. State testing and the results of these exams have in turn had wide-ranging repercussions that affect the children, the school system, and even real estate prices. Unless we correctly describe the environment in which we teach and deal appropriately with its inherent challenges, we are fighting a losing battle. The best and most powerful way for a classroom teacher to be effective is to accept reality and change his or her lens. Recognizing what you really do—you teach in an inclusive environment—and beginning to redefine yourself as an inclusion teacher rather than a general education teacher is taking the first step. New paths open and the feelings of being overwhelmed turn into feelings of hope for both you and for your students.

Why does changing the way you view your job make such a difference? Because it forces you to plan for the long term, to build a classroom infrastructure, year by year, that supports children with diverse needs and that also works for all children. When you believe you will always have children with different learning styles to teach, you know that the effort you put into designing curricular supports is an investment, not a stopgap for a unique situation. In the process you end up supporting the diverse learners, the typical kids, and yourself. You are ready for any student you are assigned to teach: no emergencies, no surprises. Over time you will become confident of your ability to reach children other teachers have not been able to reach, you will enjoy yourself more, and you will earn the respect of your colleagues, the parents of your students, and the administrators in your school.

This mindset leads you to provide supports automatically. Here's one simple example: when giving your class an assignment with written directions, you also read the directions aloud and then have a child in the class explain the assignment, following up by asking whether anyone has any questions. Spending a few minutes at the start of the assignment to make sure it is clear means the difference between success and frustration for some children, but all learners benefit. Making this key accommodation part of your regular routine supplies an essential support for some, offers additional helpful information to others, and is a signal to all that you respect the fact that students may need clarification, that they may have questions they need answered, and that this is not unusual or unexpected. And since the children know you are going to call on someone to explain the directions after you have read them, they will all listen a little more closely in case they are the one chosen.

Children who are not afraid to ask adults for help when they don't understand, who take responsibility for getting the information they need and for being a partner in their education, have a huge advantage. It is not easy for all children to do this, however, and even those who are able to ask may stop if they feel embarrassed about having to do it more than other children in the room. Providing the accommodation of repeating the directions and inviting the whole class to ask for help and clarification goes a long way toward helping all children in the class understand that asking questions and making sure they understand what is being said is part of their responsibility as active learners.

Making standard accommodations (for example, presenting new information in the context of something that is already familiar, providing information in more than one way, offering information in small chunks, and checking understanding frequently) for all children and making them permanent requires less effort in the long run, because those habits you acquire remain in place: you don't need to start from scratch every year. Children with a variety of needs are automatically supported.

A teacher building an inclusive classroom might make a habit of using the following basic lesson format:

- *Review* the previous day's material by asking questions that the students answer aloud (5–10 minutes). Alternatively, go over the homework during this time.
- *Uncover background knowledge* before introducing new material (5–7 minutes).
- *Use a mini-lesson* to present new material (10 minutes).
- *Model* the task and *ask questions* to check for understanding (10 minutes).
- Ask children to *work on the task in groups or in pairs* while you observe and talk with them (20 minutes).
- *Provide notes and study guides,* and use them for review and for reference.
- Assign homework that allows the students to *practice independently.*

If you (rightly) expect that diverse learners will always be in your class, you will consistently incorporate what they need to benefit from your daily lessons and end up benefiting all your students. A ten-minute mini-lesson rather than a twenty- or thirty-minute lecture automatically delivers information in small chunks. The format of review, mini-lesson, group work, and independent practice naturally builds on the learning of the day before and allows you to continually assess students' understanding, clear up misunderstandings, and reteach or provide extra practice as needed. After a while, this type of planning will become automatic, and you will substantially reduce the amount of potential difficulty experienced by both you and your students.

As your repertoire includes more and more inclusive practices, special accommodations for individual children will be needed less frequently, but any specific accommodations that *are* needed for a particular child can be added with much less effort. (What is more, in the interests of your inclusive classroom, you may decide to incorporate them permanently.) Incorporating supports into the structure once and for all is much easier and more effective than tinkering around the edges for years.

Once you start to incorporate the accommodations and teaching strategies outlined here, you will see immediate benefits: learning will happen more smoothly, student behavior will improve, children will begin working more independently, and classroom transitions will become more orderly. As you continue developing these supports in your classroom and adding to them over time, long-term benefits will also emerge: you will increase your ability to serve diverse needs in your classroom, your students will become more confident and skilled, and you will build a reputation among parents and colleagues as a teacher who is able to teach *all* children. You will be the teacher who can teach any child and have fun doing it.

When you construct a supportive environment (your inclusion classroom), one in which you do not have to put out the same fires over and over, not only will all students in your class thrive but you will also gain the space you need to be a reflective teacher and the time to do all you have to do.

■ Asking the Right Questions

Wait, you may be thinking, I really do have kids in my class to whom it is impossible to teach the required curriculum. Well, if you are using the curriculum "right off the shelf," you are right. Your classroom may include children with cognitive, emotional, social, and/or behavioral challenges ranging from mild to significant and impeding their academic development. For the teacher in an inclusion classroom, however, the question should be, How can I teach the curriculum in a way that will make it accessible to all the children in my classroom? To do this the teacher has to know the needs of every child in the class, needs that will differ from child to child and change from year to year. When you plan your lessons using the inclusion lens, you need to think about how to accommodate your class in two ways: (1) present the lesson in a way that all the children in the class will be able to understand, and (2) be sure that all the children in the class have the necessary skill and background knowledge. You'll then provide the opportunity for those who do not have the foundational skill or background knowledge to acquire it.

Recently, I saw this sign in a classroom:

> If Children Don't Learn the Way We Teach,
> We Must Learn to Teach the Way They Learn.

This is the essence of what you do as an inclusion teacher. When you are planning, you will be thinking about the curriculum, but you will also be thinking about how to explain a concept in another way and about having children take intermediate steps that may help them succeed. As you develop ways to accommodate students and integrate the resulting insights into your understanding of how children learn the things they need to learn, you will develop materials and strategies that will prove valuable again and again. This is a long-term approach, not a short-term fix or a teaching tip. And you know from experience that short-term fixes don't work.

■ Building a Team

Just as the inclusive structure of your classroom provides needed accommodations for children, a special education team that works well together supports your efforts and helps deliver more effective instruction to diverse learners. Some of us are lucky enough to "inherit" smoothly running teams in our schools so that kids immediately benefit from the best expertise and services. But what if the team isn't immediately working well? Team-building (or team-mending) is an important endeavor that we sometimes avoid because it can take us out of our comfort zone. Therefore, it's worthwhile to think about the barriers stopping us from having a "team made in heaven" and keeping us locked in an unsatisfying "team in name only." It's also worthwhile to consider taking a leadership role in developing the team because the rewards in terms of providing the best possible support are so great.

One potential barrier to collaboration comes from the unique environment in which teachers work. While we may share resources or methods with grade-level colleagues and consult with other teachers when we have a problem with a particular child, for the most part, we work alone. In our classrooms *we* are the final authority; we make decisions and plans, and we carry them out. In addition, few teachers have the chance to see how other teachers do their jobs or what other classrooms are like; few teachers need to integrate their teaching style with someone else's. The positive result is that teachers have developed very strong independent problem-solving skills, finding ways to make their classrooms work. But this Lone Ranger approach can be a problem when a child with a disability is not making progress, and this is where the team approach is truly required.

The teacher and the special educator both have the same objective—to provide the best possible services for every child. The best way to achieve this is to think in terms of *what we can do together.* On some teams, teamwork is defined as each person doing a separate job, like workers on an assembly line hoping to produce a good result. Even more powerful is collaborating on solutions and coming up with plans together that are better than what any individual can produce alone. Closer collaboration is always something to work toward, even as we recognize our own ambivalence about conceding some of that veto power we have enjoyed in our classroom "sole proprietorships."

A good team can provide you with the necessary tools to keep you from feeling as though you are drowning in a sea of needs. Teachers who have effective teams in place and who work in environments that support inclusion are more successful with their students, less stressed, and more satisfied with their jobs. As a highly skilled and respected teacher recently told me, "With the way things are, I am afraid talented new teachers will be burned out by the demands of the children and the curriculum and leave the profession." All progress toward removing stress is valuable.

As you build your inclusive environment and as your team becomes more effective over time, teaching a classroom of diverse learners will change from "overwhelming" to "manageable" to "stimulating and rewarding." Teachers who have instinctively embedded supports in their classrooms form more productive working relationships with the all the children in their class, and they are happier in their jobs. They're not the teachers who complain about getting "a really tough group this year"; they're the ones other teachers look at and wonder how they do it. With the right organizational mindset you can do it too, and with the help of your team, you can do it even better.

■ How This Book Works

This book is primarily for general education teachers who each day are required to teach children with a range of abilities and needs. It provides the rationale and perspective for building accommodations into the classroom structure and explains the benefits of making standard accommodations automatically available to all who need them. It shows general education teachers how to set up their classrooms so that accommodations installed once continue to benefit students year after year with little additional effort, because they are built into the classroom structure. Special educators can also use this book to support classroom teachers in their efforts to build inclusive environments and promote the benefits to the teachers and students alike. The book helps teachers take a leadership role in developing their special education team into one that offers the best education possible for all children in the class. It also provides them with an overview of some common learning challenges and the types of accommodations children with these challenges require.

School administrators concerned about supporting all those general education teachers responsible for diverse learners can use it as a basis for professional development workshops. Such sessions could help give general educators the tools to build their inclusive classrooms and to promote collaboration between general education and special education teachers.

For the same reasons, this book is also a useful addition to teacher training courses at the college and graduate levels, providing those going into the teaching profession with information they will need to successfully build classroom environments that provide support for all types of learners.

The goal of this book is to encourage and guide teachers to take the needed steps to correct the problem of *the misnamed classroom*: one that is called a general education classroom but in reality is not general education, not special education, but *inclusion,* and to counter the idea that there is a clear division between special education and general education. As a profession we need to acknowledge that in today's world we teach in inclusion classrooms containing a full spectrum of learning differences and special needs. We need to do more than just correct the name of the classroom, though. If we are to be successful as teachers and happy at our jobs, we must also make our classrooms truly *inclusive,* meaning classrooms that genuinely provide for the needs of all the children in the class

This book is comprised of three sections. Part I consists of Chapters 1 and 2 where you will find descriptions of common learning challenges and practical information (as opposed to clinical descriptions) that teachers, special educators, and student teachers can use as a quick refresher. These disability profiles can be copied and used as handouts and distributed to team members, art, music, and physical education teachers, and parents of newly identified children to establish a common understanding, create an atmosphere of trust, and serve as a starting point for further reading and research.

Chapters 3 through 7 make up Part II where the focus is on specific inclusive practices, such as how to build a classroom structure that automatically provides most of the accommodations children need, including setting up the physical classroom and the embedded routines that support diverse as well as typical learners. This section also discusses the teaching practices that help all children make progress, develop a love of learning, and experience academic success. There is a chapter on assessment and a chapter on behavior, with explanations of how inclusive practices support positive behavior in students.

Part III includes Chapters 8 and 9 and focuses on communication, with discussions on improving the team's effectiveness, taking a leadership role on the special education team, and working with the special educator to build your inclusive environment and support structure. This section also looks at ways to develop the kinds of communication skills we need to form strong alliances with parents, coworkers, and the children in our classes.

The big question this book addresses is not, "How do I survive this year with this child?" but "How can I accommodate children in my classroom in a way that will make a difference for the kids I am teaching this year and all the children—both typical and with special needs—I will be responsible for teaching during the rest of my career?" When you see the accommodations you make and the effort you put into designing your lessons, not as a special service for one child but as adaptations you will use over and over, your work becomes an investment that will provide returns for many years. The inclusion classroom will meet the educational needs of your students in the best possible way, but it will also meet your needs as a teacher—your need for immediate improvement in your ability to manage and teach your inclusion class and your long-term need to feel the pleasure that comes with knowing you have the ability to teach all children assigned to you, no matter what their challenges.

In Summary

It is good, but not sufficient, to have a perfectly prepared general education classroom. The reality is you *will* be teaching an inclusion class consisting of students with a range of abilities and learning styles.

The most important things you can do are accurately define your classroom as an inclusion classroom and yourself as an inclusion teacher, build an inclusive classroom structure, and employ effective, long-term inclusive teaching practices: *if children don't learn the way we teach, we must learn to teach the way they learn.*

Successful teachers understand they will always have children with a range of abilities in their classrooms. They build accommodations and supports into the classroom structure. These accommodations have several benefits:

- They continue to pay dividends year after year and can be added to over time.
- They are effective and invisible, available to all who need them.
- They take little effort to provide and maintain once incorporated.

Keep the range of learners' needs in mind when planning lessons. Over time, the mind-set of an inclusion teacher will become a habit, your repertoire of strategies will grow, and you will find yourself automatically considering and providing for all.

The other important component is the special education team. Remember,

- Everyone has one, but not all teams are as good as they can be.
- An effective special education team will support both you and your students.
- We need to make sure methods that work for us in one setting do not sabotage our efforts to work collaboratively.
- Building a supportive team is worth the effort as the rewards are great.

2 | A Guide to Common Disabilities

The disabilities described in this chapter are those most commonly found in classrooms today. These descriptions are windows into how children experience a particular disability. If we walk in their shoes, we will better understand why they think and act the way they do, and the power of this understanding will enable us to design solutions to the attendant problems. If we can articulate our needs and feelings as teachers, while putting ourselves in the place of these children, their parents, and their classmates and seeing the world as they see it, we will better understand what has to be done. Understanding others' reality and imagining how they feel or what their motivations are allows us to respond appropriately and give students what they need (Heward, 2005).

This section of the book began with a conversation among five people: A woman who worked as a special education advocate and who is also the mother of a child with a learning disability, talked about her experiences with teachers and school systems that did not provide students with what they needed. A graduate student in education who has ADHD talked about her experiences in school when she was growing up and how her ADHD affected both her and her mother's lives. There were two special educators who had stories about what happens when children with disabilities are in classrooms where their disabilities are not understood. I was the fifth, and as I listened, it struck me very powerfully that everyone was working toward the same goal: to do the best they could for the children they work with, but each felt they were in the battle alone. It seemed that providing insight into each perspective, describing the whole picture in one place, would be useful.

Teachers often observe certain behaviors and will say a child "has" a certain disability because of what they see in class. Other times they may observe behaviors that do not seem like a recognizable part of any known disability. While no two children are alike, the profiles presented later in this chapter attempt to demonstrate what the teacher can do when certain behaviors are seen, as well as presenting the other sides of the story in order to understand the situation better and to help avoid accidentally doing or saying something that could make adversaries out of individuals who are actually on the same side. The disability descriptions are brief and contain the essential hallmarks; they are not clinical descriptions. You can find more detailed and scientific descriptions in reference books and on the Internet (see Hallahan and Kauffmann, 2005; and Deutsh, 2006).

The parents' perspectives in these profiles come from many hours of listening to their concerns and visions during IEP team meetings, as well as other conversations about their children and their experiences. The recommendations are strategies and interventions commonly used every day by special educators and others to make and carry out individual educational plans—not all are for each child with each disability, but they all are helpful to some children with those disabilities. The recommendations are widely used and proven to help children access the curriculum. I would like to note that the suggestions and insights provided in the Autism Spectrum Disabilities section are largely based on the writing and thinking of Carol Gray and Kathleen Quill, both of whom have made valuable contributions to our understanding of children with these challenges (Gray, 2000; Quill, 2000).

For each disability, there is a list of focused classroom accommodations. While these accommodations will trigger immediate improvement and may ease much of the difficulty these children have in the classroom, each child and each situation is different. It is important to have a general understanding of the disability but also to know the individual child. After putting the accommodations in place, we must then use our knowledge of each child to design further, more individualized accommodations.

These accommodations are most effective when used in an inclusive classroom, and they involve thinking with our heart, understanding that while a child may need certain accommodations and supports to make the curriculum available to her, she wants what we all want—friendship, a feeling of belonging, and a sense of accomplishment for work well done. If these needs are not considered, if we do not develop a classroom structure that allows children with disabilities to satisfy these needs to the same degree as their more typical classmates, we will be left wondering why these children do not seem motivated to learn and do not respond to our requests as other children do. Any time we can reasonably implement an accommodation for the whole class, we should. It will go a long way toward making learning-challenged children feel accepted and included and is much easier than keeping track of special accommodations for just a few.

We should also always remember that while general accommodations work in most cases, each child is an individual. We mustn't be afraid to discontinue an accommodation that proves to be distracting or does not solve the problem it was intended to solve. We need to observe the children in our classes as they use the accommodations day by day and modify them if necessary or design new supports that will serve them better.

Developing ways to help children with disabilities in an inclusive classroom is fascinating and rewarding. In this environment, the special education team is able to analyze a child's learning needs in relation to his learning goals and implement a plan that targets his particular needs and really makes a difference. With team support and with inclusive habits and routines in place, we are able to meet students' academic, social, behavioral, and organizational needs without the added layers of stress typically present in a regular classroom.

You may copy these summaries and distribute them to parents of newly identified children, to specialists, and to paraprofessionals. Doing so will establish a common understanding of the challenges related to a disability and explain the rationale for common classroom accommodations. This understanding opens up lines of communication, decreases the likelihood of misunderstandings, and helps the special education team discuss the salient issues and make a comprehensive and workable plan.

Attention Deficit Disorder (ADD/ADHD)

General definition:

Attention deficit disorder and attention-deficit hyperactivity/disorder (ADD and ADHD) begin in early childhood, before the age of seven. The symptoms are severe and persistent, and the child must exhibit them both at home and at school. If these symptoms appear suddenly or are only exhibited in certain settings and not others, it is not ADD; the behavior change may be caused by a crisis at home, problems with the curriculum, social problems, or some other situation. The difficulties of a child with these disorders are mainly in the areas of attention span and impulse control, and if ADD is the only issue, the child should be able to learn like a typical child when the disorder is controlled through accommodations or medication. Sometimes children with ADD are also hyperactive, exhibiting behavior such as moving around the room when the expectation is that they remain seated; this is called attention deficit disorder with hyperactivity (ADHD). Children with ADD without hyperactivity are sometimes referred to as ADD–inattentive type (see www.schwablearning.org).

A teacher may see a child who:

- Appears inattentive when lessons are presented to the group
- Dives into an assignment even before hearing all of the directions
- Doesn't turn in work consistently, sometimes because it was not finished, sometimes because it was completed and accidentally left home, sometimes because she was not aware it was assigned
- Rushes through assignments, doesn't follow through, and often makes careless mistakes
- Dislikes and/or tries to avoid tasks that require him to work independently and exert sustained mental attention and effort
- Has a messy desk and often loses or cannot find work and materials
- Is subject to internal and external distractions more than most children
- Becomes easily frustrated
- Has difficulty waiting her turn, interrupts others, blurts out answers, or monopolizes conversations
- Gets out of his seat at inappropriate times or fidgets and moves around excessively when the direction is to sit quietly

A parent may see a child who:

- Is upset because she did her homework but forgot to bring it to school
- Feels as if he can't do anything right
- Has difficulty taking turns in conversations and other social situations
- Is anxious and worried about school
- Can sustain attention when involved in something she enjoys at home but cannot seem to finish her school assignments
- Daydreams
- Is enthusiastic and seems younger than his peers

Parents may be concerned that:

- Their child is disorganized and unfocused
- Their child is not completing assignments and is therefore receiving poor grades
- Their child's self-esteem is suffering

Parents may hope that:

- Their child can master an organizational system that will enable her to keep track of assignments and turn them in on time
- Their child will be more successful in school and have more self-confidence as a learner

Friends may see someone who:

- Is friendly and social
- Is creative
- Is willing to take a risk or do something unusual
- Is fast-moving and enjoys interactive games
- Is bossy

The best assignments:

- Are engaging and provide the child with a way to monitor and challenge his own performance
- Have guidelines and provisions for getting frequent feedback from an adult or a peer

Try these things:

- Seat the child away from distractions such as a talkative classmate, windows and doors, sources of noise (like heaters or other noise making mechanical devices), and shelves holding materials that can be touched or played with.
- Seat the child near the teacher and near children who are physically calm and on task, facing the teacher and away from fellow students who could be distracting.
- Provide a stable classroom arrangement. Try not to change the physical arrangement unless there is a curriculum-related reason.
- Establish a stable set of routines for transitions, such as beginning the day, changing classes, going to lunch and recess, and ending of the day. Spend time at the beginning of the year establishing these routines, and reteach and reinforce them when necessary.
- Establish a predictable daily structure. Post the schedule, including any changes, so the child will be prepared.
- Organize the classroom so that there is "a place for everything and everything in its place."
- Introduce and monitor organizational strategies.
- Be consistent with the way you give directions.
- Give directions in a list, rather than in paragraph form (first, then, next, last).
- Check that everyone understands the directions before beginning the assignment.
- Repeat directions in a matter-of-fact way. This shows you understand this is a support the child needs and makes the child more likely to ask for clarification if she is confused.
- If the child has problems turning in his homework, modify the amount of homework given so it is not overwhelming. Add more when the child is ready.
- Check in frequently to monitor progress and give feedback on progress and performance.
- Set up a procedure to help the child tolerate delayed feedback (take a number, ask a peer, etc.).
- Use a positive tone when giving feedback to encourage the child to persist in his efforts.
- Establish an acceptable way to take breaks during long tasks, such as getting a drink of water, getting up and stretching, etc.

- When possible, introduce interactive ways to practice concepts (questions and answers, interactive games).
- When you observe behavior that puts other children off, speak to the child privately about why the behavior bothers the other children and establish a nonverbal signal to cue him that he is behaving this way.
- Acknowledge that waiting her turn is difficult for her, and provide positive feedback when she does.

Nonverbal Learning Disabilities

General definition:

Children with a nonverbal learning disability (NVLD) have difficulty understanding nonverbal information; typically, their rote verbal abilities, such as using correct grammar and learning the names of objects, are not a problem. These children may learn to read at an early age and possess a vocabulary significantly above their grade level (hyperlexia). Therefore, the disability is sometimes not diagnosed until more abstract thinking is required. Concerns about children's social adjustment and ability to make friends may surface before academic concerns do. These children have difficulty with social relationships because they don't understand nonverbal communication, such as body language, facial expressions, and sarcasm. Also, their literal approach to language makes inferences and figurative language difficult for them to understand. When reading, they may pay great attention to detail without grasping the big picture. Their organizational skills are weak, and they often have difficulty with spatial tasks such as writing and mathematical calculations (Quill, 2000).

A teacher may see a child who:

- Retells a story he has read but has difficulty understanding the main idea
- Speaks rapidly in a high-pitched voice or uses an odd cadence. This is more noticeable when she is anxious
- Seems immature and dependent
- Gets upset at social interactions that are inconsequential but may not react at all when peers make a sarcastic remark about him
- Spends recess alone, possibly pacing back and forth in the same spot for the entire time
- Keeps disorganized materials and cannot locate books or papers when they are needed
- Has a wealth of knowledge about a few subjects that interest her
- Seems to prefer socializing with adults or younger children
- Has visual/spatial issues that make it difficult to line up math problems, resulting in calculation errors
- Has trouble understanding abstract math concepts
- Is thrown off by an unexpected change in routine

A parent may see a child who:

- Was average or advanced in early language development, learning to name objects and speak in grammatically correct sentences on schedule
- Can decode text that is above grade level but may not enjoy reading, unless it is about one of his interests
- Has an amazing memory for facts relating to her interests
- Returns from school and needs time alone to unwind
- Does not have much common sense
- Becomes increasingly anxious as the demands of school increase
- Plays well with younger siblings but does not often play with his peers
- Has a difficult time at social gatherings

Parents may be concerned that:

- Their child who has, in spite of social difficulties, done well with rote academic skills (decoding, straightforward computation) in the early grades is now experiencing academic challenges

Parents may hope that:

- Their child will make at least one good friend and develop the social skills to get along with his classmates and teachers
- Their child is able to use her academic strengths productively while building the ability to generalize information and increase her understanding of nonverbal communication

Friends may see someone who:

- Is "out of it" or "doesn't get it"
- Always wants to do things his way
- Seems odd and is easy to tease
- Has just a few interests
- Sometimes gets upset for no reason and at other times does not seem to notice that someone is being unkind to her

The best assignments:

- Incorporate structure to support the child

- Use the same layout or format for assignments, assessments, and independent work
- Pair a new type of assignment or new information with corresponding visual information or relate it to something familiar

Try these things:

- Maintain a calm atmosphere.
- Establish routines and schedules, with time built in for orderly transitions.
- Post the schedule for the day, so the child can check it to see what is coming next. This is also a way to let the child know in advance when there will be changes in the schedule.
- Post a list of the topics to be covered in a lesson, and check them off as you address each one.
- Allow sufficient time at the end of the day or the end of a class period for the student to write his assignments down and gather his materials.
- Give the student supports that will help him organize materials.
- Schedule regular times during the week when the student (or the whole class) can organize her desk and binder.
- If taking notes from the board is difficult for him because of visual/spatial problems, provide printed notes or copies of the overhead transparencies that were used during class.
- Give her a clear role in small-group interactions that plays to her strengths: fact finder or note taker, for example.
- For assignments that require synthesizing information or determining the big idea, provide help in the form of graphic organizers and explicit explanations.
- Provide models of what a final product is expected to look like.
- Establish clear and consistent rules for classroom interactions to help the child function better socially and ensure he is treated well by others.
- If you see the child doing something that is alienating her classmates, explain why that behavior is not working from the other person's point of view, and suggest how she might want to act in the situation.
- Devise structured situations in which the child can socialize and form relationships (for example, a weekly "lunch bunch" for practicing conversational turn taking and socializing).
- Arrange for the child to bring a friend to occupational or speech therapy sessions.

Asperger's Autism (High-Functioning Autism)

General definition:

Asperger's autism has some symptoms that overlap with a nonverbal learning disability, but it is generally considered to have more severe repercussions on a person's ability to function in school. In both, early language acquisition appears normal (unlike full-fledged autism, which includes severe delays in early speech). Children with both NVLD and Asperger's autism have difficulty understanding the theme when reading and trouble understanding nonverbal communication in social situations. However, the belief that what is in their mind is also in other people's minds is much more pronounced in children with Asperger's autism than in a children with NVLD. Children with Asperger's may not look people in the eye, may have very specialized interests, and have little interest in pretend play. They may also have difficulty integrating their senses, as children with NVLD also sometimes do (Gray, 2000; Quill, 2000).

A teacher may see a child who:

- Is rigid in his behavior and speech
- Seems to be generally uninterested in socializing
- Has difficulty with social situations
- Becomes upset when there is an unexpected schedule change
- Needs routines, needs to know what is going to happen next
- Has difficulty with abstract thought—making inferences, understanding nonverbal communication—whether written or spoken
- Enjoys drawing in an individual, stylized way
- Has unusual mannerisms

A parent may see a child who:

- Spends time alone and seems to prefer it to the company of others
- May need to unwind after school by pacing or riding on a swing
- Has strong interests in a few specific areas
- Does not seem interested in playing pretend games
- May not be very responsive to smiles or other nonverbal social cues
- Does not like to be cuddled

- Engages in repetitive physical behavior, such as hand flapping or rocking that becomes more pronounced when she is upset or anxious
- Has a tantrum for no discernable reason
- Is very sensitive to physical sensations, such as noise, touch, light, or temperature
- Dislikes changes in routine or new experiences

Parents may be concerned that:

- Their child will not develop the coping and social skills needed to become independent

Parents may hope that:

- Their child will make friends, become more able to tolerate and cope with new or unexpected situations, and be successful at school

Friends may see someone who:

- Is not interested in many types of play
- Seems different
- Is not competitive and may not understand or may ignore the rules of team sports and games
- Likes to play by himself

The best assignments:

- Include visual aids to which the child can refer throughout, such as clearly written directions and models of the end product
- Involve steps that make it easier for the child to understand and help her work more independently

Try these things:

- Provide a predictable schedule, organized assignments and materials, clear directions, and cues for when a transition is coming.
- Help the child anticipate transitions and make them smoothly.
- Build cues into class work (math class starts with five minutes of mental math and is almost over when you say, "Take out your assignment

book, and write down your homework," or, "Five more minutes to work."

- Post each day's schedule, and alert the child to changes from the routine.
- Give the child a personal schedule to carry with him.
- Help the child understand an assignment and how to accomplish the task.
- Provide clear, step-by-step directions (first, next, then, last).
- Use the same format for recurring assignments.
- Link new information or directions to familiar ones.
- Provide models of the finished product.
- Check whether the student has understood.
- Present lessons in a sequential, organized way.
- Give extra time for the child to answer.
- Refocus the child if necessary, especially during whole-group lessons.
- Provide practice scripts linked to what happens in class: how to act or what to do in certain situations.
- Use social stories (a technique developed by Carol Gray) to explain nonverbal social interactions, preview a change or a special event, prepare for a transition (a new school year, for example), or rehearse social situations.

Dyslexia

General definition:

Dyslexia is a learning disability that specifically impairs people's ability to read even though they have received good instruction and have average intelligence. It usually stems from the inability to make connections between sounds and letters and difficulty learning and generalizing rules of language (Birsh, 2005).

A teacher may see a child who:

- Refuses to or avoids reading aloud or with a reading buddy, even one who is much younger
- Does not complete her assignments
- Has trouble associating sounds with letters, which is indicated by an inability to decode nonsense words accurately
- Knows the initial sound of an unfamiliar word and guesses the rest
- Seems unable to stay on task during independent silent reading, looking at pictures, trying to get others off task, or exhibiting other undesirable behavior

A parent may see a child who:

- Says he is stupid
- Is embarrassed to be reading at a lower level than her classmates and possibly a younger sibling
- Is depressed
- Is under a great deal of stress from trying to hide his reading difficulties from his teachers and peers
- Doesn't want to go to school
- Says she hates reading
- Resembles himself as a child (if the parent also has dyslexia)

Parents may be concerned that:

- Their child will give up on school
- Their child is falling behind in content areas because she is not yet reading at grade level

Parents may hope that:

- Their child will keep up with the curriculum while increasing his reading skills
- Their child will one day read for pleasure
- Teachers recognize their child's strengths, intelligence, and talents, and give her opportunities to show them in the classroom

Friends may see someone who:

- Is artistic
- Is creative
- Is good at sports

The best assignments:

- Have clear directions written at the child's reading level
- Include required reading at an appropriate level
- Make more difficult material available via recordings

Try these things:

- Devise a nonverbal signal the child can use to indicate he is willing to read aloud, and do not call on him unless you see the signal.
- Pair the child with a classroom peer at the same reading level.
- Arrange to have the child read to a student in a lower grade, and let her practice reading the book ahead of time.
- Make sure assignment directions are at the child's reading level; if that's not possible, read the directions aloud to the class, and be available to explain them.
- Teach homogeneous, guided-reading groups strategies for decoding unknown words: breaking the word into syllables, removing the prefix and/or suffix and reading the base word, sounding out, using context, etc.
- Make sure there are interesting books available at the child's *independent* reading level.
- Keep a running list of books read to foster feelings of accomplishment.
- Give a small reward after the child reads several books at his independent level.

- Teach the child how to tell if a book is at her independent reading level (she should be able to read and correctly pronounce all words on the page except possibly unusual names of people or places).
- Find and use interesting books at an appropriate reading level, especially when the child is working with a small group.
- Make sure the child understands all written directions and required texts. If material is too difficult, provide the necessary support and accommodations.
- Have the child listen to more difficult books on tape in order to build his background knowledge and vocabulary.
- Use mini-lessons to teach phonics rules, syllable division, and word attack strategies (including using context and morphemes).
- Make sure the child is never put in situations in which she is embarrassed by her reading level.
- Provide opportunities for success at school, so the child feels he is a valued class member.

Dysgraphia

General definition:

Writing is a complex undertaking. It involves generating ideas, organizing them in a way that will make sense to the reader, using grammar and vocabulary that is somewhat different from and usually more sophisticated than speaking, spelling words correctly, and committing the result to paper either in legible longhand or on a word processor. One or more challenges in these areas can result in *dysgraphia*, or writing ability that is less skilled than expected based on children's intelligence and/or grade in school (Birsh, 2005).

A teacher may see a child who:

- Often cannot locate needed materials, books, papers, and folders
- Does not record assignments or records them incompletely
- Writes sentences that have words missing or are grammatically incorrect but can correct them when she hears them read aloud
- Spells even small, common words incorrectly and whose spelling may not follow phonological rules
- Has handwriting that is difficult to read, even for him
- Turns in little written work because writing is so arduous
- Is frustrated and fatigued by writing assignments

A parent may see a child who:

- Avoids writing tasks, either "forgetting" to do them or not allowing enough time to do a good job
- Never writes anything well. No matter how much time she puts into an assignment, the result always falls short
- Is frustrated because he cannot read his own handwriting and therefore cannot edit his work
- Is not able to spell words that she should know

Parents may be concerned that:

- Their child's spelling and handwriting difficulties will diminish what others will think of the content

- Their child's intelligence and work ethic will be misjudged by others based on the appearance of his written work

Parents may hope that:

- Their child will be able to communicate effectively through her writing—expressing what she knows and thinks in a written form that is organized, readable, and spelled correctly
- Their child will become proficient with word-processing/spell-check programs

Friends may see someone who:

- Is writing challenged but good at sports, music, art, etc.

The best assignments:

- Present each stage of the writing process—prewriting, drafting, revision, and editing—as a series of well-defined steps
- Explicitly state what is required, include planning tools to help the student prepare to write, are broken down into manageable pieces with intermediate due dates, and provide models of the finished product

Try these things:

- Make planning and prewriting tools part of every writing project.
- Break long-term or complex assignments into smaller tasks with interim due dates.
- Have the child read his writing aloud (in a whisper if necessary) to find errors.
- Assign a peer editor to read the piece to its author and make changes the author dictates.
- Have the child use the text-to-voice option on the word processor so she can hear the piece and find and correct errors.
- Make sure the child becomes proficient with word-processing/spell-check programs. (If the problems stems from muscle weaknesses, allow him to dictate lengthy assignments to a scribe.)
- Let the child use a word processor.
- Give the child extra time to complete an assignment.

- Let the child make an oral presentation.
- Assign group work in which writing tasks are shared.
- Provide opportunities to be successful and to feel like and be seen as a valued part of the class.

Arithmetical Learning Disability

General definition:

A specific learning disability in arithmetic, like all specific learning disabilities, is evidenced by lower achievement in math than would be expected based on a child's intelligence and grade level, even after factoring in a sensory disability such as poor vision or economic disadvantages.

A teacher may see a child who:

- Needs a great deal of adult assistance with math
- Does not line numbers up when doing calculations
- Cannot recite basic math facts, even after years of practice at school and at home
- Uses inefficient strategies (counts by ones rather than twos, fives, or tens, for example)
- Does badly on timed math facts tests
- Has difficulty with place value
- Has difficulty generalizing learned strategies and applying them to new situations
- Has trouble identifying the operation to use when solving word problems
- Forgets previously learned information

A parent may see a child who:

- Needs an excessive amount of time and/or help to do math homework
- Does not remember the teacher's explanation about how to do the problems assigned for homework
- Makes calculation errors because numbers are not properly written or lined up
- Does not remember the multiplication tables

Parents may be concerned that:

- Their child's slow progress in math means their child is falling behind
- Their child will not be able to catch up

Parents may hope that:

- Their child will develop an understanding of the number system and do well in math in the future

Friends may see someone who:

- Is good at literacy-based tasks
- May love reading
- May enjoy writing stories

The best assignments (see Fosnot and Dolk, 2001):

- Are challenging real-world problems whose solutions can be reasoned out using the child's level of knowledge
- Require children to share their thinking as a way to validate all strategies, help them see there are many ways to solve a problem, and help those using less efficient strategies to move forward

Try these things:

- Assign math problems that can be solved using a range of strategies.
- Allow the child to use number charts and calculators so difficulties with arithmetical operations don't prevent her from developing math reasoning skills.
- Provide opportunities for the child to work with an adult (to include reteaching and/or extra practice), either individually or as part of a small group.
- Make sure the child is working on problems in his zone of proximal development—not too easy or too difficult.
- Encourage the child to use manipulatives and draw pictures to help solve problems.
- Provide direct instruction on place value.
- Explain that it is much more difficult to solve problems if one is messy and disorganized, and be a stickler for neatness. Encourage the child to use lined paper, circle answers, etc.
- Instruct the child to say the whole problem as she figures it out ("Five times three is fifteen," rather than just, "Fifteen").
- Work only on the number facts the child doesn't know.

- Conduct a daily five-minute drill.
- Let the child use a number chart while building fluency with math facts.
- Have children work in pairs and small groups, and discuss strategies.
- Have children present the way they solved their problems to the class so everyone can see how others solved the problem.
- Have children explain how they solved the problem in writing.
- Have children record definitions, strategies, examples, and other information that helps them solve problems in a math strategy book they can refer to when they have trouble solving a problem.
- Avoid rote learning; make sure students understand the concepts that underlie addition, subtraction, multiplication, division, and place value.
- Have children explain their thinking, and value their reasoning even if a calculation error results in the wrong answer.
- Have children work in groups and devise their own ways of solving problems, and make sure the child is proficient in at least one strategy for each operation.
- Give children opportunities to be successful and feel they are a valued part of the classroom.

Tourette's Syndrome

General definition:

Tourette's syndrome is a condition, first evident in childhood, that causes a person to experience motor and/or vocal tics. This condition sometimes occurs in combination with other learning disorders such as ADHD. It interferes with a child's ability to be available for learning. The tics may be less severe at home, because the child is probably more relaxed there. Medications can make the tics less severe but do not eradicate them completely (see http://www.tourettes -disorder.com/).

A teacher may see a child who:

- Makes faces
- Shouts
- Jumps out of his seat
- Makes noises after directly being told to stop

A parent may see a child who:

- Is lonely
- Is reluctant to go to public places
- Is teased or bullied at school
- Must deal with this condition every day

Parents may be concerned that:

- Teachers understand the tics are not entirely under the child's control. Some children may be able to suppress tics for a period of time, but that may make them more violent when they start again

Parents may hope that:

- Teachers and classmates will be able to overlook the tics and get to know their child for the person she is

Friends may see someone who:

- Stays apart from the group
- Does unusual things
- Is just the same as everyone else when you ignore the tics and get to know him

Try these things:

- Offer acceptance and understanding.
- Have zero tolerance for teasing, ridicule, and bullying.
- Make sure all teachers and adults the child comes in contact with, including substitute teachers, are aware of her condition, so they will not think the tics are intentional.
- See to it that you, a parent, or the child himself tells the other students about the condition.
- Ask the child's classmates to become your allies in explaining Tourette's syndrome to those who don't understand.

3 | The Physical Classroom

The structure of a classroom affects those who go there to work and learn, making their daily tasks easier or more difficult. Successful classrooms incorporate structures that promote learning and independence and that generate a pleasant, cooperative atmosphere in which children are able to learn and progress throughout the year. The children and teachers who spend their days in these classrooms are eager to go to school each day; they retain the first-day-of-school feeling that success is possible. They look forward to being together and being productive. Successful classrooms incorporate accommodations for children with diverse learning needs so that *all* students can be as independent as possible, freeing the teacher to help children learn.

An important goal of accommodating children with learning challenges is to make it possible for them to learn independently. Think of it this way. If a person who needs a wheelchair wants to go inside a building that has no ramp, he or she must be physically carried inside and then out again by another person. If the building has a ramp, the person in the wheelchair can come and go as she pleases: she is independent. A good accommodation is like that wheelchair ramp. After being taught how to use an accommodation or shown where information is, a student can independently find what he needs and use it.

The walls are a perfect place to begin adding accommodations in an inclusion classroom. Displaying assignments and classroom rules and routines allows students to refer to this information independently. Rather than endlessly repeating yourself, you can direct them to these posted reminders of their responsibilities and the behavior you expect. I know you've heard this advice before, just as you've been advised to begin saving for retirement in your twenties, eat right, and floss your teeth every day. We all know we should do these things, know they're extremely beneficial, but most of us don't do them.

Try this experiment. Go into several classrooms and count the number of items on the wall that are directly related either to the curriculum or to classroom rules and procedures. Count definitions, formulas, examples, models of finished work, word walls, and any other information students can use to check their understanding and figure out independently how to solve a problem or complete an assignment. (Don't count inspirational sayings, general information, or student work that doesn't pertain to the curriculum. These things are wonderful as well and add color and personality to a classroom, but they are not accommodations to support diverse learners.) Now think about your colleagues who teach in the rooms you just surveyed. Most likely, the more curriculum-related and directive material on the walls, the more supportive to diverse learners is that teacher's approach.

Information should be posted as a topic is being taught and may or may not remain up for the entire year. If wall space is at a premium, you can use a flipchart to post information relevant to a lesson or a unit. At the start of any lesson, you can flip to previously presented information. When you move to a different subject, flip to different pertinent information. These pads can be stored and used as visual supports in subsequent years.

■ General Classroom Layout

Using the physical layout of the classroom to anchor accommodations provides a structure that makes it easy to add more from one year to the next. The accommodations become a normal part of the classroom and benefit all children. *These accommodations do externally what a child may have difficulty doing internally.* For example, if a child has difficulty storing and retrieving information in her brain, having a place in the room where the information is stored and easy to get to allows her to find it and use it. Organizing the classroom into areas containing certain types of information (math, writing, reading) helps children find what they need on their own.

When you set up your room, think about broad functions that are challenging for children with special needs but helpful to all. Memory is one such function, including long-term memory and working memory (the ability to hold and manipulate information and the ability to store and retrieve information in one's short-term and long-term memory). Organization is another function many children find challenging, and everything you do to support children here is very important. Working and learning in an organized classroom where everything has a logical place is extremely helpful. Maintaining focus is another function that is often challenging. Engaging, interactive activities, opportunities to work with peers, and opportunities for success help children remain focused on a task. Having these accommodations in the classroom will support children in becoming independent and successful, and they will help individuals understand the types of supports they need to be successful and that they can obtain these supports themselves.

Here's the big picture: provide a stable, organized backdrop for learning new things that supports children's diverse learning needs. In other words, the excitement should come from the lessons, not from making spur-of-the-moment accommodations or searching for needed materials. As you read the discussions of common learning challenges in this book and think about children you have had in previous classes, you will begin to identify accommodations that will most likely be needed by someone in your class every year. When permanently incorporated into your inclusive setting, these accommodations will facilitate learning for all children and help you teach more effectively. This will go a long way toward helping diverse learners access the curriculum and be independent without any further intervention from you.

The basic classroom areas are the desks or tables at which students will do their work; a place where the whole class can gather; a quiet reading area; and an out-of-the-way table where you can meet with individuals and small groups to discuss their work or provide additional instruction. Another essential component is a classroom library where children can browse and choose books for independent reading. Materials and supporting equipment for the various curriculum areas should also be in separate locations: a writing area containing writing supplies (paper, pencils, and the like), a reading area with books and other materials, and an area filled with math tools and resources.

One of the first things to consider is the light. You want your classroom to be as pleasing a place as possible in which to work and learn, so a cozy nook filled with natural light is the perfect spot for a quiet reading area where students can curl up with a book.

A larger, central area will be conducive for gathering students together to learn and share as a whole class. When you designate the gathering or meeting area, keep in mind that some children, especially younger ones, have a difficult time sitting without support. If you can, establish this area along walls, bookcases, or other sturdy structures to lean against. The children will be comfortable and able to participate, and you won't be constantly asking them to sit still. Teachers of the very youngest grades sometimes provide child-size folding beach chairs in the meeting area to help the little ones sit still (a scene guaranteed to prompt a smile from any adult observer). You can also teach children to sit with their legs crossed, not touching anyone else, facing the person who is speaking. Have them do this before the meeting starts, and establish a nonverbal prompt to remind those who begin to fidget.

With a little planning, an area can fill more than one need. The quiet reading area may also be the class gathering spot as well as a place students go if they need to work without distractions. In the elementary grades, this area can be furnished with floor pillows to make it even more comfortable and inviting.

The final thing to consider is how to arrange the desks. Clusters—four or five desks pushed together to form a "tabletop"—are most conducive to small-group sharing and cooperative learning projects. Such an arrangement also helps a classroom function in an orderly way: children can line up, turn in their papers, and so forth, by "table." If you like mixing things up and changing the way the students' desks are configured, be sure you do it on a regular basis (the first of every month, for example); knowing when to expect a new furniture arrangement helps students who are easily unsettled by change stay on an even keel.

■ Classroom Routines

Classroom routines (what students need to do when they arrive in the morning, for example) should be posted in the room. They should be clear and direct, the more specific the better. If children are supposed to bring specific books and materials to their desk in the morning, post a checklist near the door that lists everything they need. Most children will need the reminder at the beginning of the year, and some will rely on it all year. If you find yourself repeating the same direction day after day, make a sign and post it. Then if a child does not remember what to do, point to the sign instead of repeating yourself: as you move from telling him what to do to showing him how to find out what he needs to do, you are helping him develop the habit of independently checking the sign and saving yourself a moment of irritation and him a moment of embarrassment each morning.

■ Common IEP Accommodations

If you have students in your class whose IEPs indicate they have difficulty retrieving stored information fluidly, retaining information in short-term memory, or processing information quickly, there is no escape—you know you'll end up going over the same things again and again, but the following accommodations will help:

- Maintaining word banks
- Handing out reference sheets
- Pairing auditory and visual information during presentations
- Providing class notes
- Checking in frequently to ensure understanding
- Devoting extra time to these students

For example, if the class is studying geometry (which many districts begin teaching in elementary school) and students cannot remember how to find a perimeter, they need to know they can go to the math area and find the definition of the term in the word bank and examples of finding perimeter on a reference sheet, along with a drawing showing what perimeter looks like. Copies of math handouts and overheads used during class (either kept in a master notebook in the math area or provided as a personal notebook to every student) can serve as your class notes. With this information, children will likely be able to answer their questions and solve a math problem independently. They don't have to ask you for the information repeatedly or pretend they remember how to do it because they are embarrassed to admit they don't.

Of course, you could also prepare all these materials and give them only to the children whose IEPs indicate they need them, but then the other children in the class will not benefit (they too can use this information to become more independent). And if the students to whom you've given these materials lose them or leave them at home, they will need to ask for your help or try to fake it. Isn't it much better to prepare materials once for the whole class, in a form that can be used year after year, than to recreate them each year and keep track of them for individuals? You'll have a much better return on the same amount of effort. The great thing about incorporating accommodations into the class structure so they are available for anyone who needs them is that it accommodates cognitive challenges and supports students' independence in ways that are both effective and invisible.

Figure 3.1 lists common accommodations often found on an IEP. Some are teaching strategies, like previewing vocabulary. Some are physical supports, like a graphic organizer or a word wall. Some apply only to a specific child, like preferential seating or extra time to finish tasks.

Figure 3.1 *Common IEP accommodations*

Teaching Strategies*	Physical Supports That Encourage Independence*	Individual Accommodations
Break down multistep directions and complex language; use clear, sequential verbal directions.	Provide visual models along with auditory information (written directions, examples).	Preferential seating.
Preview vocabulary.	Set up a word wall (alphabetically grouped words that relate to the curriculum) or word bank (a recipe-type file of classroom words and definitions, a personal compilation of difficult words, or a list written on the board for students to refer to during a particular assignment).	Extra time in which to finish tasks or tests.
Introduce comprehension strategies.	Provide story maps and other graphic organizers that aid comprehension.	
Provide step-by-step directions.	Distribute checklists itemizing multiple or multistep tasks.	Allow wait time when asking questions.
Check understanding frequently; ask students to repeat the directions.	Limit the amount of material on a page.	Check in with a particular student after giving directions, especially if they are long or complex.
Read and clarify test directions.	Separate written directions into step-by-step bullets.	
Rehearse a composition orally before writing down the words.	Provide graphic organizers that capture writing elements.	
	Provide an AlphaSmart keyboard for long writing assignments.	
	Provide examples of writing assignments that can be used as models.	
Edit writing for grammar.	Activate word processing software's text-to-speech feature. This is a feature on some word processors where a computerized voice will read what the child has written, exactly as it was written, and allows the child to listen to make sure his writing makes sense and to hear and correct errors in spelling and grammar.	

continued

Figure 3.1 *Continued*

Teaching Strategies*	Physical Supports That Encourage Independence*	Individual Accommodations
Limit auditory and visual distractions.	Provide a place in the room that is relatively distraction free.	Establish visual or verbal cues for modifying behavior and/or refocusing attention.
Supply students with class notes.	Distribute handouts or copies of overheads used during class.	Establish acceptable ways to take a break or move around during class time when necessary.
Preview material to increase students' ability to participate; review material and provide extra practice opportunities to help students gain mastery.	Arrange desks in clusters to accommodate small homogeneous and/or heterogeneous groups working together or with an adult.	Offer one-on-one or small-group instruction.
Provide concrete examples of math concepts.	Use math manipulatives.	
Provide supports for spatial challenges.	Offer students large pencils, graph paper on which to line up math problems, lined paper for writing assignments.	
Provide supports for graphomotor challenges.	Let students use thick pencils, pencil guides, a keyboard, or a tape recorder.	
Create reference and strategy books containing previously learned material.	Provide master versions of reference and strategy books, in each curriculum area, for the whole class to use.	
Set up a calendar or some other organizational system to keep track of long-term assignments and coordinate the transfer of material between home and school.	Make a class assignment book or assignment calendar part of the daily routine.	

*These accommodations and strategies are beneficial to all learners.

■ Math Accommodations

The accommodations listed in Figure 3.2 satisfy many common math IEPs and provide suggestions as to how to incorporate them into the permanent structure of your classroom in a way that fosters independence and that you can use year after year. As you work with specific lessons and deal with the needs

Figure 3.2 *Accommodations to satisfy common IEP requirements for math*

The Learning Challenges	IEP Requirements for Accommodations	Add These Permanent Accommodations and Make Them Available to All
Memory, Auditory Processing	Provide reference sheets and/or class notes	Post formulas on the walls as they are taught, provide copies of overheads as class notes, prepare reference sheets and student handouts.
Auditory processing, receptive language disorders, memory, distractibility, disorders in the autism spectrum	Provide step-by-step directions for multistep tasks	Provide strategy sheets that give methods for solving word problems, plotting coordinate graphs, etc., using words and pictures to be kept in students' math binders or a classroom reference book.
Dyscalculia, Memory (long-term memory, working memory)	Provide calculators, number charts, number lines	Have calculators and number charts available, teach use of open number line, and have directions for this available in a classroom math binder or individual math binders
Language deficits combined with strong visual/spatial skills	Provide manipulatives for math	Stock an area in your room with various math manipulatives including but not limited to geometric shapes, counters, blocks, color tiles, and fraction circles.
Belief that one is "bad" at math	Provide opportunities for success	Plan lessons with tasks that are leveled, and call the ones everyone can do "challenging," those that are a bit harder "very challenging," and the extension activities "most challenging."
Challenges with vision, spatial organization, and graphomotor difficulties. Also helpful for autism, ADHD, or other diverse learners who are easily distracted or overwhelmed.	Provide graph paper for math	Have a spot in the math area where you stock graph paper, lined paper, rulers or straight edges. Also provide worksheets in a larger font and with fewer problems per page.
Memory challenges; processing difficulties; attention issues; language-based disabilities	Step-by-step instructions; break complex directions into smaller steps.	Personal math binder or folder containing strategy sheets, directions, definitions, and examples of how to solve problems. Also keep one in the classroom as a reference in the event someone leaves theirs at home.

continued

Figure 3.2 *Continued*

The Learning Challenges	IEP Requirements for Accommodations	Add These Permanent Accommodations and Make Them Available to All
Difficulties with mathematical reasoning; challenges shifting psychological sets to the appropriate procedure	Post math strategies	Teach strategies for math and have children share the strategies they use. Post general strategies and entry points to problem solving such as using benchmark or "friendly numbers" (10s, 100s, 25s, doubles), look for a pattern, make an organized list, work backward, draw a picture, act it out. These strategies can also be included in the children's math binders or folders.
Auditory processing challenges, autism spectrum disorders, language-based disorders, anxiety disorders.	Pair visual models with oral descriptions.	When explaining what you will do or cover during a class period, pair it with a visual by writing it on the board as well so students can refer to it. List jobs students must complete during a class period as well as what they should do if they finish all assignments. Use an agenda for the class period listing the activities that will take place. Another important way to do this is to provide an example of the finished product with a verbal explanation of what children are required to do—save student work to use as an example (of great, good, and needs improvement end products) that children can view and examine as they are doing their work.

of your particular students, you will come up with additional supports specific to your curriculum and classroom. Children whose primary learning styles or strengths are visual/spatial, bodily/kinesthetic, or logical/mathematical will find many of these math materials and supports helpful and will enjoy using them.

The following basic classroom supports should be part of the math area (Armstrong, 1999; Hallahan and Kauffman, (2005); Heward, (2005). Figure 3.2

lists learning challenges you will see year after year, the accommodations you may be required to provide by students' IEPs, and ways to permanently incorporate these accommodations into your classroom so they are automatically available to students. Do this work once; make the supports available to all, and both you and your students will find math more enjoyable and less stressful.

You have most likely provided at least some of these accommodations in the past. From now on, save them and incorporate them in your classroom setup. As you look at the lists of learning challenges and think about the children in your classes, you can see how an organized approach to building your classroom accommodations will pay off for multiple students over the years, giving your room the feeling of a learning laboratory as children seek out what they need in order to do the work you assign, and how their confidence grows because they can do it independently.

The following list includes teaching strategies that support diverse learners in math:

- Providing opportunities for extra practice to those who need it
- Linking new information to previously learned information (leading children to discover and verbalize the relationship between multiplication and division, for example)
- Teaching children to use strategies that call attention to visual details (such as circling the sign before beginning a problem if the child is impulsive, disorganized, or distractible, for example)

These strategies should be posted after they are taught, so you can silently remind children to use them by pointing to them, and children can refer to them when needed.

■ Reading Accommodations

Students who have difficulty with comprehension often have a cognitive style that makes understanding information in isolation difficult. Their IEPs frequently include the following accommodations:

- Activate background knowledge.
- Preview vocabulary.
- Link new information to previously taught material.
- Teach strategies for summarizing (who, what, when, where, how).
- Teach story mapping.
- Reading aloud, modeling, and explicitly pointing out thought processes related to comprehension, such as making connections, visualizing, predicting, questioning, and inferring.

Figure 3.3 *Accommodations to satisfy common IEP requirements for reading*

The Learning Challenges	IEP Requirements for Accommodations	Add These Permanent Accommodations and Make Them Available to All
Dyslexia, comprehension, language-based disabilities, autism spectrum disorders	Provide a range of texts at the student's independent reading level.	A basket or shelf of high-interest/lower-reading-level books that children can independently browse through and choose from
Comprehension; language-based disabilities, autism spectrum disorders	Teach and use pre-reading strategies, such as doing a picture walk, looking at the cover, reading the back cover blurb, making a prediction.	To activate prior knowledge, provide a pre-reading checklist (see the example in Figure 3.4) introduced in a mini-lesson and then prominently posted.
Language-based disabilities, comprehension, autism spectrum disorders, memory.	Link new information with familiar or previously learned material; teach and use active reading strategies.	Bookmarks containing reminders of good reading strategies (see Figure 3.5 for an example); provide sticky notes to mark passages in the text.
Comprehension, memory, language-based disabilities, nonverbal learning disabilities	Teach and use active reading strategies.	Sticky notes to mark interesting passages in a text
Language-based disabilities, comprehension, slow processing, memory.	Preview vocabulary.	Word bank or word wall containing vocabulary that has been taught and/or previewed
Comprehension, language-based disabilities, autism spectrum disorders	Explicitly teach comprehension strategies.	Reading strategies introduced in mini-lessons and then prominently displayed or included in a class notebook
Strong visual skills paired with language-based disabilities, nonverbal learning disabilities, processing, memory	Teach the use of and provide graphic organizers as a way to aid comprehension.	Make available a variety of graphic organizers, including story map graphic organizers, storyboard organizers, Venn diagrams, organizers for setting, character, plot, and theme.
Dyslexia, comprehension, attention.	Provide access to grade-level texts using assistive technology.	A tape player and plenty of books on tape (some teachers in the lower grades ask parents to tape themselves reading their child's favorite book)
Reading comprehension, autism spectrum disorders, memory, processing	Provide models of end products, pair verbal descriptions with physical models, provide examples of excellent, good, and poor products.	Readers' notebooks containing written guidelines for participating in readers' workshop, writing a reader response letter, and preparing for a book discussion. Fountas and Pinnell's *Reader's Notebook* (Heinemann, 2006) includes these guidelines and more.
Dyslexia, comprehension	Help children locate books that are of interest to them and develop their identity as a reader.	Book reviews written by the children for their classmates after they finish reading a book

Figure 3.4 *Prereading strategy checklist* (Fountas and Pinnell, 2001)	**Figure 3.5** *Example of a bookmark with reminders of good reading strategies*
• Look at the cover. • Read the book jacket or back-cover blurb. • Read the first pages to make sure it is "just right" (no more than two words you don't know). • Do a picture walk. • Make a connection. • Make a prediction.	**My Bookmark** When You Are Reading, Remember To . . . Make a connection (to yourself, another book, or the world), Visualize, Ask a question, Make a prediction (check to see if your prediction was right), Make an inference (check to see if your inference was right).

Many of these strategies must be taught explicitly and then practiced with texts at the students' instructional and independent reading levels. The goal is to teach and reinforce the strategies good readers use, benefiting all students.

Reading is the most important skill a student must master in order to be successful in school, so the reading area should be thoughtfully planned and stocked. One of the most important things children with reading disabilities need is to read books at their independent reading level. If students are able to find appropriate books, they won't continually choose and abandon books that look interesting but turn out to be too difficult for them. It is both an art and a science to find books that are both interesting and written at a lower reading level, especially for students in the higher grades; however, it is the key to their development as readers.

A good classroom library can be built over time. Sources for acquiring books at little or no cost are retiring teachers, yard sales, and friends with grown children who may have children's books they no longer need or want. Having a wide selection of authors and genres is important: fiction (all varieties), poetry, stories about people from other cultures, reference books, how-to books, books of puzzles and riddles, and books about animals, science, and faraway places. Dictionaries (standard and rhyming), thesauruses, and children's magazines should also be included. Books can be grouped by author or subject and at a range of reading levels, so every child in your class will have appropriate books to choose from. An alphabetized list of titles by reading level has been compiled by Irene Fountas and Gay Su Pinnell on the web at www.FountasandPinnellLeveledBooks.com or the printed version, *The Fountas and Pinnell Leveled Book List, K–8* (2006).

In addition, the reading area of the room should include the accommodations shown in Figure 3.3 (see Armstrong, 1999; Birsh, 2005; Hallahan and Kauffman, 2005; Heward, 2005.

■ Writing Accommodations

Writing is a one of the most complex academic tasks we ask our students to perform, and it is extremely difficult for some children. Writing involves organizing your thoughts while physically forming legible letters and putting them on paper. Since written language is not quite the same as spoken language, children must, at the same time, make decisions about grammar and style. The accommodations in Figure 3.6 are commonly used to help children with organizational and/or language-based learning disabilities and are attractive as well to children who like to learn using their verbal/linguistic intelligence.

Figure 3.6 *Accommodations to satisfy common IEP requirements for writing*

The Learning Challenges	IEP Requirements for Accommodations	Add These Permanent Accommodations and Make Them Available to All
Organization, language-based disabilities	Provide graphic organizers for writing.	Graphic organizers on which to capture brainstorming: organization; graphic organizers to plan the piece of writing
Memory, organization, language-based disabilities.	Provide checklists for working through multistep or complex tasks.	Post a list of steps to take when producing a piece of writing.
Memory, organization, language-based disabilities.	Provide editing checklists for spelling, capitalization, grammar, adding detail, descriptive language.	Provide a series of editing checklists for first reading, second reading, peer editing.
Various disabilities	Specific accommodations listed in the IEP.	Special writing paper, thick pencils, pencil grips, word processor, keyboard, slant boards, and other writing aides

As you teach writing strategies and techniques, summarize the important points from mini lessons and post them on the wall. For example, if you are working on adding dialogue to a story, the class can brainstorm more interesting ways of saying "he said" (he stated, cried, exclaimed, whispered, etc.) while you create a list to which your writers can refer. Or you can introduce various "hooks" with which to start an essay (set the scene, ask a question, give a definition, make a strong statement, etc.). As part of your writing instruction, you should also teach the class how to use the accommodations shown in Figure 3.6 (Armstrong, 1999; Birsh 2005; Hallahan and Kauffman, 2005; Heward, 2005.

The following supports are important for all students, not just those with learning challenges:

- Dictionaries
- A thesaurus
- A word wall (lists of "tricky" words, for example) to help children become better spellers
- A file of story ideas and "starters" for children who are having a hard time deciding what to write
- Examples of good writing in various genres

■ Multiple Pathways of Intelligence

We know from the work of Howard Gardner that we all have distinctive learning styles and that while we may have a preference about how we receive or communicate information, most of us are able to adjust to another style when necessary. For students with challenges though, adjusting is not so easy and in some cases may not even be possible, which is why presenting lessons that appeal to more than one of the senses and giving students opportunities to express their knowledge and understanding in more than one way is so important. When you allow children to receive and deliver information using all their senses, you increase their engagement and interest, because they are able to use their preferred learning style.

Think what it is like for a man who moves to the United States but cannot speak the language. He is forced to communicate in pantomime supported by the few words he may happen to know. What he can communicate is limited. In his own country, speaking his native language, he may have had a professional job, loved to debate friends about politics and philosophy, and been known as having a great sense of humor. If you meet this man when he first arrives, you will not know how intelligent or funny he is. Your communication will be basic and concrete. When you allow children with challenges to communicate in their "native language"—that is, give them a range of options by which to communicate what they think and know—you may be surprised by what is locked inside. As you begin to think more and more inclusively and realize the benefit of multisensory learning experiences, you will come up with more ideas and add to them year after year.

Howard Gardner (1999) describes seven preferred pathways of intelligence:

1. Verbal/linguistic—words
2. Logical/mathematical—numbers and what they mean
3. Visual/spatial—pictures
4. Bodily/kinesthetic—movement
5. Musical—music/musical patterns
6. Intrapersonal—self-reflection
7. Interpersonal—interaction with people and/or the environment

We know from experience that children learn most easily when they are engaged and interested in what we are telling them. Most lessons we teach in school lean heavily on the verbal/linguistic and/or the logical/mathematical pathways. If one of these is a child's strong suit, she probably is engaged in the lessons, feels successful, and enjoys school. But if we can add the other, less common pathways, more children in our class are likely to feel that way.

Start adding more opportunities to learn using the underrepresented pathways. For example, you can show pictures or a film (visual/spatial), add hands-on activities (bodily/kinesthetic), have children work in small groups (interpersonal), and ask students to write a reflection (intrapersonal). Mnemonics or songs that help children remember facts will especially appeal to those with a strong musical intelligence. Group discussions, buddy reading, or solving problems with others will be particularly interesting to children with a strong interpersonal intelligence. Tasks that ask students to make connections to their personal lives or to reflect on something they have read or learned will be enjoyable to intrapersonal learners. Building models or drawing pictures will allow learners with a strong visual/spatial intelligence to shine. Allowing bodily/kinesthetic learners to build something or demonstrate what they know by acting it out engages this type of learner and provides an appropriate outlet for his or her type of intelligence. Children with musical intelligence may write a poem or song when they are allowed to express themselves in their preferred way. Presenting information and accepting work done in a student's strongest domain holds interest and improves behavior. Students will learn more easily and begin to develop the self-image of successful learners.

In Summary

Accommodations are required by law for children with IEPs. Many of these accommodations are related to the physical room. When we make them a permanent part of the classroom setup, they support diverse learners, are good for all children, and support us as teachers by making the necessary accommodations both invisible and effortless.

Since you will probably have some students every year with the most common needs, the most labor saving thing you can do is incorporate as many of the common IEP accommodations into the physical structure of your classroom as possible.

We all have a preferred sensory pathway for taking in and giving information. Most of us can switch to a less preferred one when necessary. Children who for cognitive or physical reasons cannot switch between these pathways must be approached through their preferred pathway in order to be able to access information. When you plan your lessons with this in mind, they will become more engaging for everyone in your class.

If you give students a choice of how they express their understanding, you will be able to assess more accurately what they have learned. Students that previously have had difficulty fully expressing what they know will have opportunities for success that will build their confidence and self-image as learners.

4 | Curricular Supports and Accommodations

If you don't know where you're going, you'll end up somewhere else.

—Yogi Berra

Have you heard this joke? One person says to another, "I've been teaching my dog to speak French." The recipient of this information is very impressed: "That's amazing!" The first person replies, "Yeah, I just keep wondering when he is going to learn it." If we teach something, and they don't learn it, did we really teach it?

Educators are under pressure to teach a broad curriculum and to have their students do well on standardized tests. But racing to cover the curriculum whether the kids learn it or not is not what the administration, the parents, or the children really need from us. We are in control of the curriculum; it can't accomplish anything without us. We can use inclusive practices to make sure it doesn't go too fast, isn't too demanding, and doesn't remain out of some students' reach. Anyone can stand in front of a class, present lessons out of a book day after day, assign the next chapter for homework, continue to plow through the material, ignoring the fact that some students simply do not understand what is being taught.

■ An Instructive Fable About Instruction

Every day in the staff lounge you have seen a colleague knitting. You have watched with fascination as simple balls of yarn are transformed into elaborate sweaters, mittens, and hats. Her knitting needles fly, and you can tell by watching her it is an activity she enjoys. When you ask about it, she tells you knitting is something she does while watching TV or talking with friends. She loves it because she finds it creative, relaxing, fun, and rewarding. She enjoys making gifts for people she cares about, and she loves having the ability to make herself articles of clothing that are the perfect color and style. This sounds wonderful, and you want to learn how to knit too. She agrees to teach you; she tells you she has taught many people, and they all can now knit just about anything they want.

Excited, you buy your supplies and meet her the next day for your first lesson. You're lucky; you've found a good teacher with a method that yields excellent results. First, she has her students become automatic with the basic stitches of knit and purl. They practice until they are able to recover if they drop a stitch and can knit with consistent tension, so their measurements will be correct. They learn how to read the pattern, sew the knitted pieces together, and block the finished garment. She always has her students start by making a plain scarf; then they move on to afghan squares in different patterns of knit and purl stitches. When she feels they're ready, she lets them make a sweater. Her students grow to love knitting. It becomes a fulfilling, enjoyable hobby. Sometimes they come back and show her things they have made years after they stopped taking lessons.

But imagine that at your first lesson you tell your colleague you want to make an intricate fisherman's knit sweater covered with several kinds of cables and bobbles. She tells you it is not an appropriate project for a novice like you. You beg her. You tell her you have already bought some expensive yarn and have chosen the pattern. You offer to pay her for teaching you, three lessons a week, forty-five minutes each. She reluctantly agrees. You start right in with your sweater project. Actually, she starts the sweater for you, and she knits the first few rows while telling you what you need to do. You listen and pay attention; things are going fine—and then she hands the needles to you. You get three quarters of the way down the next row when you lose your place and drop a stitch. You don't realize it until two rows later when the hole in your sweater shows up. You are devastated. You thought you were doing really well, and now all that work was wasted. Your lesson is almost over. Knowing how hard you worked and how bad you feel, she picks up the dropped stitch for you and corrects your mistake while you watch with relief. She tells you to knit ten more rows before your next lesson.

When you get home, you start right in on your homework. You do what you think she said to do, but your stitches don't look the same as the ones you did with her. You do it anyway and bring it in next time. It's not exactly right, but she fixes it for you and says it's time to start knitting the cables and bobbles. You can't read the pattern, so she tells you what it says and shows you what to do. She sits right next to you as you knit, watching, advising, helping you over the hard parts, and cheering you on. You have a neighbor who can knit, and you ask her to help you with your homework. She is not as patient as your teacher, and sometimes she just does the knitting for you. All of your knitting is done with someone else, during your lessons and at home. You do feel you are learning and getting better, but you only knit when someone is there to help you, and you would never just drop everything and knit.

Nevertheless, the weeks go by, and your sweater begins taking shape. It does have a homespun look, but it definitely looks like a sweater. You notice your teacher's other students have completed scarves and are working on their afghans. They seem to find knitting fun. You don't really understand that; for you it's practically the opposite. Knitting is stressful, and sometimes concentrating that hard for an extended time gives you a headache. Maybe you were just not meant to be a knitter.

Many months go by. At last your sweater is finished. You definitely know more about knitting than when you started, but you cannot knit on your own, and you would never think of doing it for fun or relaxation. You don't understand why anyone feels that way about it. You put your knitting needles away. And that's too bad. If you had made scarves until it became so automatic you could make one while watching TV, and then, step by step, added to your skills, you might now find knitting fun, creative, and relaxing—everything you dreamed it would be.

■ Make a New Plan, Stan

You were hired to help your students learn a body of knowledge based on your district's goals and curriculum, but most likely you were not told what to do when some children don't learn the material or how to scaffold the curriculum for children with diverse learning needs. There *is* a way to teach every child in a diverse group of students, but to do so you need to start the year knowing where you are, the range of skills the children in your class possess, and where you want to be in June. When planning lessons, you need to keep the needs of the entire class in mind—the academically capable, the average, and the challenged. Here are some basic steps you can take:

1. At the beginning of the year, assess the entire class in the major areas of reading, writing, and math. You need to know the strengths and challenges of the individual children as well as the general strengths and challenges of the class as a whole. You also need benchmarks from which to monitor the progress of your students.

2. Review the initial assessments and determine whether the whole class needs to practice a certain skill or skills. For example, you may decide

to have your class solve a math word problem and/or edit a grammatically incorrect sentence every morning to develop their skills in these areas.

3. Look at the curriculum you are to teach. What district learning goals must be met in June, and what material will be assessed on any state-mandated tests? Determine what key understandings you are required to teach and what core knowledge and skills children need to acquire in order to be successful next year. Children who are academically behind and/or have learning challenges must learn these foundational skills by the end of the year, in some way. Kids with more severe disabilities will need to "overlap" as much as possible with the mandated curriculum (Kluth, 2003). Depending upon the severity of the disability and the course work, at times you may need to provide a learning experience that allows a child to take part in a lesson in a way that is appropriate for him. This can be something like having a specific role as part of a small group, such as illustrator for a reading group. The ideal situation is when his role results in a product that makes a contribution and is aligned with the student's individual learning goals; however, at times that may not be possible, and a parallel learning experience needs to be provided.

4. Now take your knowledge of your class and your knowledge of where you need to be at the end of the year and make a map of how you will get there, defining the step-by-step increments in your daily teaching. For each unit in the curriculum, determine whether your students, wholly and as individuals, have the skills and/or background knowledge needed to understand what you are about to teach. If not, provide it. Taking the time to review the material children need to know and preview the vocabulary they will hear saves time in the long run and increases the effectiveness of your teaching.

5. Create appropriate flexible groupings based on the children's needs, the subject, and the unit. If you are working on calculating division problems, for example, you might set up homogeneous groups, one group working on number facts and one or two ways of dividing two-digit numbers, another group devising ways to solve division problems in more complex ways using larger numbers. All the children are thus developing the math skill of division, but at their own level. At other times, you may ask heterogeneous groups to work on a word problem, suggesting various methods and discussing which ones are most effective. Your ongoing assessments will help you form a variety of collaborative structures throughout the year.

6. At checkpoints during the year, reassess all your students, compare the results to the initial benchmarks, and monitor their progress toward their goals, fine-tuning your instruction as necessary.

■ The Learning Zone

We know from the work of Vygotsky (1998) that the best level for engagement and learning is the point at which the student is about 80 percent successful, a window of opportunity Vygotsky calls the *zone of proximal development* (ZPD). This is the children's instructional level of difficulty, used to plan for classroom assignments where children are working in class, together with a partner or in groups, when you are circulating around the room, talking to children, noting areas of difficulty, and providing support when needed. At this level, children have just the right amount of challenge—not too easy but doable with appropriate effort and support. Homework assignments—opportunities for children to practice what they have learned—should be such that students can work *independently* with a 95 percent or better likelihood of success. (These figures are comparable with those used to determine instructional and independent reading levels.) Homework that is too difficult to accomplish without significant parental support does not achieve its intended purpose.

Learning takes place in the classroom in many ways: group work, projects, inquiries, and experiential learning. In an inclusive classroom, where supports are available and the lessons are planned with all children in mind, these learning situations allow children to operate in various modalities, and they work very well for diverse learners. In every classroom, however, there are also times when you may want to directly impart information to the whole class. For children with attention, focus, memory, and many other challenges, this is often the most difficult format in which to learn. In a diverse classroom, the best way to provide this type of instruction is by using mini-lessons to teach a small chunk of information at a time and then giving students an opportunity to practice. This keeps the teacher talk down and the amount of time spent actually working on a concept high. Try to develop a style that imparts clearly, in easy-to-follow language, what the children need to know; answer questions, and then get on with solving problems, writing essays, or reading stories, being available to check in with and help children as needed. Children remember best what they both *do* and *say*, so the mini-lesson, followed by *doing*, with time left at the end of the lesson to *say* what they learned, is the best format. Do not let the mini-lesson become a maxi-lesson cutting into the more valuable do and say time.

This way, the information that you want to directly teach is presented in manageable chunks, with time allotted for children to gain experience and add to their skills bit by bit, much better than a long presentation that gives more information than they can absorb. Teaching in this way can help a variety of children learn and progress and makes it much easier for diverse learners to keep up with the rest of the class.

Let's say you are using group work, projects, inquiries, experiential learning, and mini-lessons, and you are assigning appropriate, worthwhile homework, but some children still don't turn in their homework. They may be having difficulty copying it down, may not remember the instructions, or may not have the materials they need at home. Your personal website is the perfect place to add routine supports, like listing each night's assignments and the necessary instructions. If you don't have a website, take a few extra minutes as students are recording the assignment and packing up for home to make sure everyone has the needed materials and understands what is to be done.

■ A Curriculum Accessible to All

A child with learning challenges in a general education classroom who is expected to do work beyond his capabilities may learn, but he probably won't develop a love of learning or the ability to work independently. This is an essential reason for a multilevel curriculum that matches the range of skills of the students in the class. When each child's goal is placed on a continuum, each new task building on the one before, she is able to work independently. As her skills grow, she will begin to understand and experience the joy others get from reading, writing, investigations, experiments, and/or doing mathematics.

The good news is that if you've set up an inclusive physical environment, you're halfway there. You just need to design your lessons so that each child can work independently when needed. How do you find the time? By establishing a structure. The best and easiest structure to implement is reading, writing, and math workshops (Atwell, 1998; Zemelman, Daniels, and Hyde, 2005; Calkins, 2006). Workshops allow each child in the class to be challenged at his or her particular level. The most important thing is to teach children the routines and tasks that make up the workshop. For any grade, you should prepare a menu listing the range of tasks the children might work on during the week.

One attribute of true workshop-style teaching is that we train kids to work on their math, writing, reading, or science *for the whole time*. We don't just give them one task which they finish and then are "done." Instead, we inculcate the norm of continuous working. If a child finishes one piece of writing, they immediately start another. If a child finishes a book, she's not "done" with reading workshop for the day; instead, she can write a review of the finished book or select a new one and start reading.

Of course you may occasionally need options for the children who truly finish early: they need to know where to go and what to do. For example, if a second grader has finished everything on the menu, perhaps he may choose among reading a book of his choice, listening to a book on tape, following written directions for making an origami animal (or drawing one), reading a magazine in the class library, writing a letter to a grandparent or other relative, or making as many words as he can out of the letters in *Happy Halloween*. A posted list of things children may do that are appropriate for the grade level (and the specific students in the class) when they finish their menu tasks keeps them engaged in workshop activities for the entire period. (A second-grade teacher I know designates Friday "ketchup day"; her class is delighted at the bewilderment of parents and visitors, who don't realize it's the day they "catch up" on the work for the week.)

Workshops are automatically geared to the individual: each child is reading, writing, or doing math at her level, his level. The teacher presents a mini-lesson to the class or a small group and delivers individual instruction in conferences and interacting with each child as he or she is working. Let's look at the three main kinds of workshops individually.

Reading Workshop (see Fountas and Pinnell, 2001)

Your goals for a daily reading workshop are for children to:

- Develop their reading skills.
- Read a wide range of texts, genres, and authors.
- Connect what they read to themselves, the world, or other texts.
- Develop a love of reading.

Each child should have the following items:

- A reader response journal. This is for to-and-from communications between the teacher and the child about the books the student is reading. The teacher asks questions and makes comments that expand the child's thinking, skills, and interests.
- A reading folder or notebook. This will eventually house an annotated list of books the child has read, a list of books the child wants to read, and any reference materials the teacher has handed out (directions for participating in a book discussion, writing a reader response, etc.).

A reading workshop includes but is not limited to the following activities:

- Reading books independently that the students have selected themselves
- Presenting mini-lessons on the routines and jobs in reading workshop
- Exchanging letters (between students and teacher and back again) about books the students read
- Having small groups of children reading and discussing the same book
- Discussing, as a class, books the teacher has read aloud or all the students have listened to on tape
- Writing journal responses to books the teacher reads aloud in class
- Conducting small-group guided reading, assessments, or conferences

Writing Workshop (see Atwell, 1998; Fletcher and Portalupi, 2001; Calkins, 2006)

These are your goals for children in a daily writing workshop (lasting at least an hour):

- Develop their writing skills
- Produce various types of writing—essays, memoirs, poetry, journal entries, etc.
- Use writing to express themselves
- Use writing to communicate with others
- Develop the feeling that writing is enjoyable and useful

Each child should have these items:

- A writing folder. Here children keep the pieces of writing they are working on (including prewriting and planning notes, drafts, and current versions) and pieces of writing they started and put aside to be finished later.
- A writing notebook. This houses material to consult when planning or starting a writing project. It will eventually contain resources the teacher hands out in mini-lessons and other segments of the workshop, ideas for future writing projects, quick-writes in response to prompts, etc.

During writing workshop, children explore the writing process. They plan, write drafts, revise their work, solicit peer responses, confer with the teacher, and, with promising pieces, complete a careful final edit and enjoy seeing their work "published" (read aloud and discussed with the whole class). In this inherently individualized structure, all children are selecting their own

Figure 4.1 *Writing process progress chart*

Plan	First Draft	Own Edit	Peer Edit	Teacher Edit	Final Draft	Publish
Will Dan	Stephanie	Julia Sam		David	Nick	Monica	Grace

*Names can be written on clothespins or on tags attached with Velcro or magnets.

writing topics and will be working on skills and strategies that fit their unique needs.

An easy, visual way to monitor each child's work is to make a long rectangular poster that chronologically lists each phase of the writing process above a Velcro or magnetic strip. Then have each child affix their name tag under the stage they're working on (see Figure 4.1). This chart is a management tool for children who use it to guide them through the writing process, and for you, allowing you to see at a glance what part of the writing process a child is working in. It is useful in many ways: If you want to check in with a particular child the next time she is editing a piece of writing, do it when her name is under "Editing." If a child's name is under a phase for a long time, you can check in with him. Maybe Dan's name has been under "Plan" for two days. You may want to check in to find out if he is finding it hard to settle on something to write about and is planning and then abandoning idea after idea. Perhaps he is stuck and doesn't know what to do about it, or another possibility is that he is working away, making a good plan, and not in need of any help at all. The chart gives an indication of who may need a check in or a bit of help. It also helps you anticipate bottlenecks. If you see six children are about to need a "Teacher Edit," and you already have a list of four, it may be a good idea to remind the class that when they get to Teacher Edit, they add their name to the list, put their piece in the Teacher Edit basket, and then start to work on something else, putting their name on the chart in the appropriate spot.

Even the youngest children can work through the writing process independently. The key, again, is to teach what each phase entails, support kids through all the steps, and have the relevant materials on hand (graphic organizers, rubrics, editing checklists, paper, writing implements, glue sticks, scissors), so children know what to do, where to find the materials they need, and where to find answers to their questions. You can make a rule that if they have a question, they ask a classmate before they ask you. Some teachers even use the rule: "Ask three before me!" This will give you more time to meet with individual children to discuss their writing projects.

Writing workshop may include (but is not limited to) mini-lessons on the following routines and strategies:

- Using prewriting tools to plan your writing.
- Writing a lead that will draw the reader in.
- Narrowing the focus of the writing to a small "slice."
- Using descriptive language to make a picture for the reader.
- Using descriptions of how things look, feel, taste, smell, and sound to add interest.
- Rereading and revising as you go.
- Paragraphing.
- Writing topic sentences.
- Using tools such as spell check, a thesaurus, and the dictionary.
- Writing memoirs, personal narratives, poetry, fiction, journal entries, letters.
- Giving and receiving feedback.

Math Workshop (see Burns, 1992; Hiebert et al., 1997; Van De Walle, 2001)

Your goals for a math workshop (daily, or once or twice a week in connection with daily direct instruction) are for children to accomplish the following objectives:

- Develop math reasoning skills.
- Solve problems in ways that make sense to them and show their understanding of the process.
- Realize that there is more than one way to solve a math problem.
- Develop fluent calculation skills (addition, subtraction, multiplication, and division).
- Acquire an understanding of their specific math curriculum.
- Develop the feeling that math is fun.

A math workshop is the perfect vehicle for teaching new concepts and providing extra practice opportunities to students who need more help and offering extension activities to those who need more challenge. You may want to present a whole-class lesson in which students work together in pairs or small groups to obtain solutions using several strategies. As children share the strategies they used and explain their thinking, you will see which children are using less efficient strategies (counting by ones, drawing pictures) or are totally confused. During your opening mini-lesson in the next day's math workshop, you can have children share their strategies and/or explain the more efficient approaches and then set the class working on tasks that offer review, practice or opportunities to extend their skills while you confer individually with students or small groups of students who need it.

Math workshop activities may include (but are not limited to) the following:

- Presenting mini-lessons on routines and strategies
- Practicing concepts currently being taught
- Playing math games
- Developing math fluency
- Practicing a variety of calculation methods
- Solving word problems individually or with a partner
- Writing an explanation of how a problem was solved
- Making posters depicting math concepts
- Working on math challenges
- Working in small homogeneous groups
- Working in small heterogeneous groups

■ What Most Becomes a Teacher

Curiosity about your students is the best stance to take; this will positively affect both your ability to understand them and the level of success they are able to achieve. By observing students and analyzing their work, you will discover their strengths and weaknesses, where they need help, and when they need to be challenged. As you walk around the classroom, you will ask them about the assignments they are working on and what their thinking is. Talking and corresponding with each child one-on-one, you will develop an understanding of what they need as learners and as people and be able to infer why they do the things they do and what kinds of supports they need.

If a child in a classroom does not seem to care about doing her work, many teachers are quick to label her as lazy; others take it personally and become angry; still others become annoyed at her lack of cooperation. But if you believe there is a way to reach each child, you will be curious about why this student is apathetic or rebellious. Are there times when she does care? If so, under what conditions? As you talk to her about her thinking and correct her work, you'll look for clues. Eventually, you'll come up with a plan for turning the situation around.

In Summary

Assessments at the beginning of the year give you a picture of the range of skills in your class and any gaps that need to be filled. If the class needs it, schedule short daily practice sessions involving the necessary skills.

Examine district goals, and compare where your students are now with where they need to be in June.

When teaching new information, take the time to activate the prior knowledge your students need to understand the material and preview any new vocabulary they may not know.

Use workshops to provide effective and appropriate instruction to every child in your class. Workshops allow you to differentiate instruction, provide one-to-one help, assess how children are doing throughout the year, and make sure everyone is on track.

Believe there is a way for each child to learn, and be curious and dedicated enough to find it.

5 | Classroom Climate

This chapter is mostly about practical ways to build a supportive, friendly, interdependent classroom group. But first, let me take a minute to review the way that some students come to us with particular labels—a condition which especially challenges us to include them educationally, socially, and personally in our classroom community.

By law, before you can recommend that a child be evaluated for an IEP, you must discuss the child's challenges at a meeting of other faculty members (sometimes called a *child study group*), brainstorm ways to help him, and try these suggestions in your classroom. (If a parent requests an evaluation, this requirement is waived.) If the child fails to respond, the child study group may (with his parents' consent) refer the child for testing. Over the next few weeks, a battery of standardized assessments will be administered to try to determine whether his problems at school are caused by a learning disability. Sometimes the testing will clearly reveal a significant disability. Other times, the results are not conclusive. A child may be having evident difficulty, but there is no compelling evidence of a learning disability. However, without inclusive structural supports, he will fall further and further behind. So we all have students, both labeled and unlabeled, who need our careful support.

It can be challenging to integrate accommodations into a regular classroom. The accommodations must not only fit many different children's needs but also be applied consistently; if they are simply plopped into an environment not generally supportive of diverse learners, they probably will not work. Both the teacher and the child end up feeling even more insecure.

But when you change your lens—take the attitude that learning must work for all—and build supports into the structure of your classroom, the situation isn't so tough after all. It is then a relatively easy task to add the accommodations that will make a difference. Here are some suggestions for helping the children with learning needs in your inclusive classroom:

- Repeat directions and important information: tell the class what you are going to tell them, tell it to them, then tell them what you told them.
- Ask children to repeat directions back to you, so you are sure they understand.
- Write directions on the board as you say them.
- Format written directions in a step-by-step list, not as a run-on paragraph.
- Put daily homework assignments on your website or on a recording reachable through your phone extension; children who need a reminder or who were absent will have a quick and easy way to get the information.
- Assign children a homework buddy who will check whether they have recorded the work correctly in their assignment book at the end of the day, and whom they can call in the evening if they get confused.
- Post a calendar in your room that indicates holidays, special assemblies, the starting dates for new units, and due dates for long-term assignments and all intermediary steps.
- Have each child maintain a math notebook containing math aids, math vocabulary definitions, practical problem-solving information, and examples.
- Set up a take-a-number-please or sign-up system for children who need your help while they are working independently, so they can continue to work while they wait their turn.
- Schedule some movement into the day—going from sitting at desks to meeting on the rug, working in small groups, moving from one work station to another.
- Give credit for and feedback on both process and product.
- Send a postcard home telling parents something good their child did that day.

As you incorporate these inclusive routines and supportive habits, you will see positive results. Don't be too hard on yourself or on your class; habits take time to establish, both for you and for the children. Incorporate changes in routines at a comfortable pace. Taking small steps is fine as long as you are still moving forward.

Also, when establishing new routines, it is important to keep trying. When something doesn't turn out as planned, remember you are developing knowledge and skills by attempting, reflecting, adjusting, and trying again. When you habitually think about supporting all types of learners and incorporating accommodations that increase your effectiveness and the likelihood that all children will be successful, the ratio of "good days" to "bad days" will increase, and the severity of the tough ones will decrease for both you and the students.

Understanding what diverse students experience in the classroom leads to new ways of thinking about the curriculum and planning lessons. As you set up your classroom to support all learners and cultivate an inclusive mindset, your efforts will become more and more effective. You will find that within this structure, you can do what you do best: teach and engage children with your own style and your own personality. These are some of the positive results:

- More engaging lessons. You may develop and present interesting, real-life problems and situations.
- More successful group work. Children will be able to work in pairs and in small homogeneous or heterogeneous groups much more efficiently. You will have more opportunities to talk with children about their thinking and perform other types of informal assessments.
- More time in which to plan and assign challenging work and to modify assignments to accommodate those with the highest and lowest skills. Each child encounters tasks with appropriate demands and thus remains actively engaged, experiences success, and makes progress.
- More time in which to provide feedback aimed at helping every child build on what he or she knows in order to understand more and become more skillful.
- A feeling that the class is a special community. Hand-tailored classroom rituals, unique ways to celebrate work well done, special names for classroom routines, all make being in your class a memorable experience and contribute to the feeling of unity.

■ Being Yourself

As you set up your systems and procedures and plan your lessons, what you are really doing is developing your own style as an inclusion teacher. Inclusion teachers come in all varieties. Some are sweet, some are gruff.

> I have been going to school now for six years. Some of those school
> years were soft and gentle, and some were hard, cold years. It de-

pended a lot on the kind of teachers I had. It also depended on me. The best year so far is this year. This year has a good heart. And that's because the heart of this year is Mr. Larson. (Clements, 1999)

If you've read *The Landry News* by Andrew Clements, you know Mr. Larson is not a perfect teacher, but he has lots of good qualities. He is reflective, doesn't hold a grudge, has respect for his students, and he provides experiences that are real, complex, and interesting. There are many jobs to do in the classroom, and all the children take part to the best of their ability. But most of all, Mr. Larson's students understand that their teacher has a good heart. That is what really matters to kids—and that is the beginning of a positive classroom climate.

You do not have to be funny or be an entertainer or know how to play a musical instrument to be a good teacher. When kids know you are on their side and like them for who they are, warts and all, they will like you for who you are, warts and all, right back. In an inclusive classroom, all children, including those with IEPs, feel they are important and welcome and able to succeed every day. The structures and habits you establish will make your classroom safe, collegial, and supportive for all (even the most able children worry about failing). Diverse learners will progress at their own pace, and the typical and advanced children at theirs, all with appropriate support. Your class will run more smoothly, and everyone will be ready to learn.

Teaching is a profession that requires you to be your authentic self, but that can be very hard to do when you are starting out or implementing a new method. While you are finding your way, it is more than okay to replicate the techniques you read about or others give you. Get as much advice and help as you can: it is all valuable, especially when given by talented teachers who have had successful careers and can give you many tips.

Successful teachers have developed a unique style that makes them memorable to the children lucky enough to be in their classes. Some of their ideas may work well for you too, but not all of the specifics may translate. Maybe you're a forty-five-year-old woman who became a teacher after many years in another career, and you're trying to emulate the style of a twenty-eight-year-old man who began teaching right out of college. The ideas make sense, look like fun, and work great for him, but when you try them, the fit isn't quite right. Maybe you adapt them to make them your own, maybe you find other ideas that work better, but you're thankful for the tips.

When you discover a great strategy, use it; then reflect on what worked, what didn't, and how to make it your own. Remember what it feels like to start something new, because that's what changing to inclusive teaching is. It's hard in the beginning, but it gets easier. Keep this in mind as you take courses and read books, including this one, and begin to incorporate various ideas into your teaching practices.

■ Expectations, Tolerance, and Accepting Differences

High expectations have a huge effect on student achievement. We've all read articles or seen movies (*Stand and Deliver* is one) about educators who have accomplished great things in their classrooms because it never occurs to them that their students might fail. I love classroom posters that state the teacher's high expectations for the class or ask children to have high expectations for themselves. But over time I've concluded that while high expectations are necessary, we need to communicate these expectations in the right way. Tolerating and accepting cognitive and learning differences is every bit as important as having high expectations.

Beneficial high expectations result from the following ideals:

- Presenting achievable challenges
- Providing the tools and support students need to meet these challenges
- Believing you can teach all the children in your class everything they are required to learn
- Being willing to use a different instructional strategy and/or develop an alternative assessment of a skill when appropriate

Having high expectations for your students and a commitment that you will do what is necessary to help them meet those expectations shows your students that there are two sides to the pact. They become more actively engaged in learning and begin to understand their role (to construct knowledge for themselves) and their responsibility (to ask for the help they need when they need it), and we provide the support they need. As these subtle messages take hold and children demonstrate their ability to measure up to expectations—their own, their teacher's, and their classmates'—they develop increasing confidence in themselves as learners.

There is another form of high expectation—the "cheerleader" type. This is easier to implement, but it is dangerous, particularly in inclusive classrooms. Teachers who believe in this kind of encouragement are always surprised when it doesn't work. They use it in good faith, believing it will help their students rise to ever greater heights. They tell their students, "I know you can do it!" convinced that this will make the difference. And maybe it will, if all the students have the knowledge and tools to solve a difficult problem and the innate tenacity and confidence to keep trying until they succeed. Otherwise, it is doomed.

Cheerleading is most risky in classrooms that include students with learning differences and challenges, because it is one sided. The implicit message is, *I have presented the material and given you directions. My job is done. You should be able to do this work if you really try.* There is no corresponding expectation the teacher has to meet. When children fail, the blame falls squarely, and only, on them.

The damage failing to meet these expectations does to children's self-confidence and their sense of being part of the class is compounded if the teacher becomes annoyed. This loudly and clearly states that there is one way to learn, and if you are unable to do it, you have disappointed your teacher. Children feel the others in the class see them as a failure, and they begin to see themselves that way as well.

Imagine if it happened to you.

What if the principal of your school gave all the teachers a computer disc containing a tutorial and told you each to create a classroom web page to add to the school Web site, everything to be up and running in time to be unveiled at the PTO meeting the following week? Within a few days, all of your colleagues have installed serviceable web pages that have all the required features. However, you've never done anything like this before and, if you're honest, admit to being a technophobe.

You work really hard on yours, but when you upload your page and click your name on the menu, nothing happens. You ask other teachers for help, but they're busy and tell you everything you need to know is in the tutorial. You keep trying, but the day before the deadline, you have to tell the principal you need more time. He rolls his eyes, and word gets around that the reason the new web pages can't be announced at the PTO meeting is because yours isn't working. Last week, you thought of yourself as an intelligent person who just wasn't good with computers. Now you feel a whole lot less intelligent and competent than everyone else.

What went wrong? The principal's expectation motivated you to try hard, but you started from less than zero. You had less experience and ability in this area than the rest of the faculty. When you ran into difficulty, the principal's expectation didn't help you accomplish the task. You needed *a higher level of assistance*. If he had said initially, "I will make sure you have all the tech support you need to learn how to do it," would that have made a difference? Of course it would, because the responsibility would have been shared, as it should be. Expectations are important, but you also need the necessary tools, instruction, and assistance.

That this kind of experience has the power to make us question our ability and self-worth is something to think about. If this had happened to someone else, you would have told your colleague it wasn't his fault: "It doesn't mean you can't learn it, it just means you need more help." But none of that mattered when it happened to you. The reaction of the principal and the fact that your colleagues knew about your ineptitude made you feel even worse. You were letting everyone down, including yourself. (And even getting the thing to work eventually wouldn't help very much—too little, too late.)

Children feel the same way, and these feelings have a big impact on how they see themselves and how they feel about school. Having a teacher who is intolerant of cognitive differences can be devastating. A teacher who appears annoyed or upset with a child who cannot do the work or is unable to focus or exhibits any other kind of uncontrollable behavior is making a negative judgment. The judgment is very apparent to the child and to the rest of the class and sends a powerful negative message.

Year to year, children show observable differences in achievement depending on their teacher's tolerance for their learning style and on the accommodations the teacher supplies. In extreme cases, vulnerable children can be made to appear much more severely challenged than they are, a cause for misery all around. Understanding and accommodating disabilities goes a long way toward reducing feelings of impatience and helping us better support our students.

All children want to do well in school. Teachers who believe everyone belongs provide children with individually appropriate expectations and give them the tools and information they need, which when combined with the children's own effort leads to success. They accept children as they are, determine their needs, and supply the supports necessary for the children to be successful. Defining yourself as an inclusion teacher and learning what it takes to make appropriate accommodations gives you the tools be one of those teachers. It gives you permission to let children progress from where they are. Together, you and your students will then celebrate successes and approach any problems as something to be analyzed and collaboratively solved.

■ Self-Assessment

It's easy to read about how to be a great inclusion teacher and become excited about the ideas; it's a lot harder to map a path from where you are to where you want to be. The assessment in Figure 5.1 is based on my observation of a number of educators, all of whom were dedicated inclusion teachers. It's not comprehensive—it's an initial screening meant to help you think about different aspects of your job and figure out where you are on the road to becoming a teacher who uses inclusive practices and is able to connect with and teach

Figure 5.1 *An inclusive-teacher assessment*

Circle the one description in each row that best describes you.

Great (3 points for each one circled)	Good (2 points for each one circled)	Needs Improvement (1 point for each one circled)
You have a great deal of tolerance for different learning styles and special needs.	You are tolerant of different learning styles and special needs.	You have little tolerance for different learning styles and special needs.
You believe accommodations are necessary for some and good for all.	You are willing to use an accommodation when a particular child needs it.	You believe some accommodations give children an unfair advantage.
You use paraprofessionals to help children advance their skills.	You use paraprofessionals to help children complete assignments.	You use paraprofessionals to keep the classroom running: control behavior, organize materials, etc.
You have a clear and detailed knowledge of each child's strengths, weaknesses, and learning needs.	You know where each child falls in the class hierarchy. You know the needs of the lower third of the class.	You know the weaknesses of the poorer performing students in the class.
You analyze curriculum in relation to a continuum of knowledge and what you know about the children in your class, then plan your lessons accordingly.	You sometimes adapt some lessons for some children in the class.	You use the curriculum as it was written and seldom make changes for a particular student.
All kids—typical and those with special needs—hope to be in your class.	Children are happy to be in your class.	Special-needs children and their parents may find being in your class difficult.
You really like every child in your class; while you see similarities to other children you have taught, you view each one as a unique and interesting person.	The children in your class are great; you get a handle on them quickly because you have had similar children in your class in previous years.	Most of the children in your class are great, but there are some who definitely rub you the wrong way.
All children in your class are successful every day.	Children in your class are successful at least half the time.	There are some children in your class who are rarely successful.

Highest score = 24

all types of learners. It's also meant to help you see that small changes in out-look, added together over time, make a big difference in how you define your-self, how you do your job, and how effectively you function in a classroom of diverse learners. When you implement inclusion practices—and the habits that go along with them—in your classroom, you will see automatic changes in your profile. Keep in mind that all habits take time to establish but once established become automatic and are effortless to maintain.

While your score on this quiz is certainly not scientific, it might be a good way to start thinking about where you are on the path toward becoming a full-inclusion teacher. It can also be useful to take this quiz with a group of col-leagues and talk through the questions and implications together.

■ The Classroom Community

Accommodations that are well integrated into the classroom structure become invisible. In a classroom set up for inclusion, children with diverse needs do not stand out; the supports help children succeed academically without making them appear different and possibly getting in the way of collaborative learning relationships. Children who succeed socially as well as academically are in-vested in being a part of the class, which is the best motivation to behave well and exert themselves. Children who feel supported, who know the tasks they are given are appropriate and attainable, and who have warm relationships with their classmates and their teacher like school and enjoy learning. In con-trast, a child who feels like an outsider will not like school and may either shut down academically or be disruptive.

Making sure children form friendships and are accepted by their peers is as essential to their academic success as giving them preferential seating, step-by-step instruction, or extra time to finish a task. The proof is all around us. Adults who enjoy their work and their peers are much more likely to be suc-cessful than those who hate their job and count the minutes.

Part of our responsibility as teachers is to make sure every child in the class-room is safe, both physically and emotionally. While all children (and all adults too, for that matter) need help with relationships now and then, some chil-dren have more difficulty forming friendships than others do. Most teachers and parents agree that if a child is friendly with all her classmates (that is, if no one is bullying or teasing her, and she is not bullying or teasing anyone) and has one or two good friends to sit with, talk to, and play with, she is on firm ground socially. As teachers, we need to take notice of children who are being teased or bullied. These children may be introverted and have a hard time making social connections, or they may have learning differences that make their behavior seem different or odd.

Classroom rules are the first step in establishing a positive culture in which students are safe and friendships can flourish. These rules, based on the golden rule (treat others as you would like to be treated), should be discussed with and agreed to by the children. Indeed, many smart teachers negotiate classroom rules and procedures with students, rather than posting teacher-made regulations at the start of the year. With bigger kids, you can make a project of writing a Classroom Constitution—a nice combination of social studies content and group development (Beane, 2005). Whatever process you use to ensure student cooperation, it's important to post the resulting rules in the room: often, disputes can then be settled by the children themselves, who use the poster to determine when a transgression has occurred.

Unfortunately, we can't assign a friend as we can assign a reading buddy, but there are many things we *can* do. Dr. William Glasser (1992), whose work is the foundation for the Creating the Peaceable School program, states that all behavior is motivated by four basic needs: (1) the need to belong, which is fulfilled by caring, sharing, and cooperating with others (in the higher grades this is manifested by dressing in similar ways and liking the same music); (2) the need for power, which is fulfilled by achieving, accomplishing, and being recognized and respected; (3) the need for freedom, which is fulfilled by making choices; and (4) the need to have fun, which is fulfilled by laughing, playing, and experiencing enjoyment. An inclusive classroom makes steps toward meeting these needs.

Cooperative learning projects are a very effective way for children to interact, work together, and get to know one another. Ensuring that every child in the room at some point works with every other child fosters the feeling that the class is a group in which everyone is an equal member. Establishing classroom routines and unique celebrations and activities make the classroom feel like a family or special club.

The need for freedom is satisfied because there is no one right way to solve a problem or do the work. In the inclusive classroom, children can show what they know and share their strategies and thinking in a variety of ways. This adds to the feeling of being a community of learners who work together, listen to one another, and learn from one another.

The need for fun is met when lessons are engaging and interesting: incorporating many styles of giving and receiving information.

But an inclusive classroom makes the biggest difference in satisfying the need for power. Typical learners usually have no trouble feeling recognized for a job well done, but diverse learners don't experience such recognition unless structures are in place to support their needs and guarantee their success. When children aren't successful academically, Glasser states they may try to fulfill their need for power in the following ways:

- Bossing other children around, always insisting things are done their way in the classroom and on the playground
- Taking enjoyment from pointing out someone else's mistakes
- Monopolizing conversations and/or bragging about what they have or things they've done
- Teasing, bullying, or starting rumors about other students

Looked at this way, this sort of inappropriate behavior can be seen as what it is: children's attempt to satisfy their need for power and feel better about themselves—a futile attempt that is bound to fail and quite possibly harm other students.

When students are recognized for making progress at their own rate and moving forward, several things happen. First, they are no longer motivated to satisfy their need for power in undesirable ways. Second, they begin to work harder on assignments and value the progress they make toward achieving their personal goals. Third, their image, in their eyes and the eyes of their classmates, changes from that of a troublemaker and a slacker to that of a learner. When the need for power is fulfilled, children can begin to form relationships that turn into friendships.

■ Promoting Friendships

Since we have established that friendly relationships are important to children's academic success, it follows that teaching children how to form productive and satisfying friendships is something we should spend time on. From the beginning of the year on, it helps to have a class meeting every week or two. (These meetings don't have to be long; fifteen or twenty minutes are usually sufficient.) At the first meeting, the class should establish the rules for their classroom, as discussed earlier. The rest of the meetings become forums in which to address conflicts and discuss what it means to be a friend and a member of a learning community.

A good way to begin a discussion of friendship is to dispel some of the myths surrounding it. Ask your students to take the quiz in Figure 5.2. When you discuss the results, emphasize that making friends takes time and that many people need only one or two good friends. Sometimes children worry that they

> **Figure 5.2** *Friendship, true or false*
>
> It is easy for most people to make friends. T F
>
> It is important to have a lot of friends. T F
>
> People can always tell right away if they are going to be friends. T F
>
> True friends never disagree or argue. T F
>
> If you have friends, you never feel lonely. T F
>
> Being best friends means you are always together. T F
>
> It is important to have friends that are popular. T F
>
> Your friends should like you for who you are. T F
>
> You can have more than one good friend. T F
>
> Some people like having a lot of friends. T F
>
> Some people are happy with just a few friends. T F
>
> Making friends takes time. T F

Answers: F, F, F, F, F, F, F, T, T, T, T, T
Based on information at The United States Department of Health and Human Services Web site at http://mentalhealth.samhsa.gov/publications/allpubs/SMA-3716/making.asp.

are the only ones who have difficulty making friends, and it is reassuring to know that others face the same problem.

Next, ask your class what they think makes someone a good friend and record their answers on chart paper, sharing the things you value in your friends as well. Here are some possible responses:

Good friends:

- Smile at each other and have a positive attitude
- Have a good sense of humor
- Have similar interests
- Share their things with each other
- Give honest compliments
- Show that they like each other by listening to each other and sharing things about themselves
- Invite each other to do things or go to each other's house
- Spend time with each other

After you talk about this list, ask the students what kind of person they would *not* want to be friends with. Here are some possible ideas:

People who would not be a good friend:

- Are mean or bullies
- Always have to get their way, are too bossy
- Make jokes about others and laugh at them
- Exclude people from games or groups and try to get others to do the same
- Brag and show off
- Have a negative attitude and bother other people when they are trying to work
- Are copycats, try to act like you instead of being themselves
- Lie, cheat, or steal

To have a friend, you must be a friend. During your periodic class meetings throughout the year, continue this conversation about relationships. You can talk about problems as they arise, and the children can discuss solutions in a neutral, nonthreatening atmosphere and in general terms, no names mentioned. Many activities and suggestions for promoting friendships can be found at The United States Department of Health and Human Services Web site at http://mentalhealth.samhsa.gov/publications/allpubs/SMA-3716/making.asp.

Although you can't just tell children to be friends, if you see a friendship beginning to blossom or feel two children would be compatible, you can arrange for them to work together in the classroom a bit more than usual, thus giving them more time together to interact and to get to know each other. You can also let parents know whom their children are friendly with in school; the parents might then arrange after-school or weekend activities with their children's friends.

Some children simply may not know how to broach friendship and may need more help. Perhaps they are very shy and need encouragement. Or perhaps they have some degree of autism or have difficulty interpreting nonverbal communication. If children are being treated by the school's speech and language pathologist, perhaps the pathologist can set up periodic "lunch bunches" to help these children increase their social skills. During a group meeting, talk about how to approach someone you would like to know better. One of the simplest ways to show you would like to be friends with someone is to smile at them. Have children turn to the person next to them and say, "Hi, can I join your game?" first with a scowl, then with a neutral expression, and finally with a smile. Ask them how they felt after each invitation—did the person's facial expression make a difference?

Asking children what they like to do to relax and have fun can help them figure out what they want in a friend. It's also good for them to think about which activities are more fun with another person and which are better done alone, and what possessions they may not want to share. Thinking about the things they enjoy doing may also prompt them to come up with new activities they would like to try.

Speech and language pathologists or guidance counselors often use the following approach to teach children how to start conversations:

- *Give a compliment:* "That's a cool t-shirt" (perhaps it has a picture of a sports team or a musical group).
- *Then ask a follow-up question:* "Have you ever gone to one of their games (concerts)?"
- If the child responds yes, *make a positive statement:* "That must have been fun. I'd like to hear about it."

This strategy should prompt several back-and-forth exchanges, and practicing it with the teacher can make it easier for a shy student (or one with a nonverbal learning disability) to approach another child.

During your class discussions on how to be a friend and keep a friend, make the following points:

- You mustn't take friends for granted. You need to show your friends you care about them.
- Friends listen to what they say to one another and share things about themselves: what they like, what they think, what is happening in their lives.
- Close friendships develop when you like other people for themselves, not for their possessions or because they are popular.
- You need to spend time with friends. Try to think of fun things to do with your friends outside school.
- It takes time to make a friend; friendships get stronger over time.
- It's okay if your friends spend time with other people; you have to give them space.
- It's great to make new friends, but be sure you keep your old ones too.

Discussions like these provide a basis for dealing with relationship difficulties in general and those between specific children. Having an established framework will help you determine whether the problem can be alleviated by changing the way you deliver your instruction (giving students more opportunities to experience success, for example) or by reminding specific children how friends behave with one another.

In Summary

Establishing the habits and routines of generosity and acceptance in a classroom is essential. They take time to develop, but once they are established, they are easy to maintain.

The supportive and inclusive climate and accommodations established in a classroom will help all children, not only those with an IEP.

We need to have high expectations that our students can succeed and correspondingly high expectations for ourselves as teachers who are able to help them succeed.

Friendships are essential if children are to be successful in school. As teachers we must provide an environment in which all children are emotionally safe and where friendships can grow.

Ongoing discussion of and work on friendship issues is an important part of the classroom culture.

"Behavior Problems": What Our Students Are Trying to Tell Us

6

One of the hardest parts of teaching is dealing with disruptive behavior. The rhythm and atmosphere of the classroom is thrown off when a teacher needs to redirect students' attention or intervene to keep the class running smoothly. Rules with attendant punishments after a certain number of violations are cumbersome at best and insensitive at worst. While they may work for a while, they are not a permanent solution: they don't address the reasons for the undesirable behavior (Kohn, 1999).

One of the best ways to promote positive behavior in the classroom is to make sure that the same intrinsic rewards are available to everyone. Knowing they are able to meet expectations and succeed motivates students to focus on their work rather than on ways to avoid it. When students do not experience the natural rewards of being in school, the artificial rules and rewards we devise are never as effective as getting to the root of the problem and adding supports. No reward we can provide can match the glowing feelings of being successful, being a part of a learning community, and having the respect and friendship of one's classmates. As teachers, we want the positive behavior of the children in our classes to be voluntary and self-rewarding, not motivated by the possibility that they may lose recess.

We know from experience that all behavior is communicative. Without our having to say a word, our glassy eyes and unenthusiastic body language let a friend know that we've seen enough of his vacation photos. The children in our classrooms communicate with us continuously via their behavior, both as a group and individually. An elementary school teacher knows better than to stand in front of the class and lecture for an hour: her students cannot pay attention that long. After a while their whispers to their friends will announce, *we can't do this anymore*. When individual children act in challenging ways, they are often telling us they are having difficulty with what they are being asked to do. It may also be an internal problem that we need to understand and address. But these are only general statements; it's up to us to discover the specific problem and what we need to change or provide.

Setting up a classroom that supports everyone is the most effective way to teach, and it is also the most effective way to turn a child's challenging behavior around. Classrooms designed to support diverse learners and a curriculum that provides every student with opportunities to be successful every day have the added benefit of decreasing disruptive behavior. Spending your days without ever experiencing success while your peers do is demoralizing and antithetical to learning. We want to empower children to be learners, but unless we make sure all of them are successful and view themselves as able learners, their motivation and their behavior may well deteriorate.

Imagine that you have a job you must go to every day. You cannot be fired, and you cannot quit. You started the job with hope and the certainty that if you worked hard, you would do well. Over time it has become clear that no matter what you do or how determined you are, you just are not able to do good work. Sometimes you think you've done something right only to be told later that you missed part of the directions or did not do enough. Your coworkers whisper about you, you see your boss alternately trying to hide her pity and her irritation. Your family and friends say it can't be that bad, you just need to try harder. Maybe you joke about it to make it clear you don't care, or maybe you become so depressed that you shut down.

Many children are in just this situation. The first day of school is filled with hope and excitement, but this feeling can quickly wear off, replaced with the certainty that the hope they had was foolish and nothing will ever change. We have the power to prevent this from happening in our classrooms. We are responsible for educating *all* our students no matter their skill level, meeting them where they are, and supporting their progressive improvement.

■ "Why Do You Do the Things You Do?"

The first thing to do in helping children who are exhibiting behavior challenges is break the code—unravel what they are trying to tell us about their school experience. When we change their experience, they will change their behavior in order to communicate that new experience. Their changed behavior lets us know our intervention has been successful.

The chart in Figure 6.1 is a general guide to typical student behavior. It lists a continuum of student actions, along with the message those actions might

Behavior	Basic Meaning	Experiences and Feelings
Figure 6.1 *Some typical classroom behavior and what it means*		
Is attentive to lessons, follows directions, does careful work, often goes above and beyond on assignments.	I love school (or at least know I am able to succeed there). I am confident I can do the work assigned, and I know I have the ability to do it well.	I get good grades and feel successful. Teachers smile at me and seem to like me. I get positive feedback on the work I do, which motivates me to continue working hard.
Is attentive to lessons, follows directions, does careful work.	I like school. I know I can do the work, and I like doing a good job.	My grades are okay, although sometimes I work really hard but don't get the same recognition the "smart kids" do. The teacher seems neutral toward me: I don't get strong positive or negative feedback. I feel like I am doing well enough.
Is attentive at least half the time, follows directions but at times needs reminders, turns in work but does the minimum.	It is hard for me to be here, but I am trying.	I worry about school all the time. The work is really hard. I get a lot of negative feedback because my work is not up to par. Once in a while I get positive feedback for something I've done but not too often. The teacher always seems to go back to being upset with me. I want to do well, and everyone says I should be able to. I hope that I will be able to do better next time.
Is inattentive and possibly disruptive during class, needs constant redirection, often does not turn in assignments.	I hate school. I used to try, but what for? The work is too hard. I would rather my teacher and classmates think I am a troublemaker than have them know I can't do the work.	I can't do the work. If I hand something in, it is going to be wrong. I have stopped trying to do my school assignments. I am now just trying to protect myself and survive. I am always making my teacher mad, sometimes when I don't even mean to. I am so far behind everyone else, I have given up hope.

be sending. Improving behavior should be noticed and appreciated; worsening behavior can be rerouted. It is unlikely someone will go straight from hating school to loving it, but progress along the path shows that things are moving in the right direction.

Children who present consistent and protracted behavior challenges have been communicating *I hate school* (and all that means) for years. Experiences like these may have brought them to this point:

- They rarely experience academic success and feel "stupid."
- They do not have any close relationships or friendships with other children.
- They do not have a good relationship with their teacher.
- They often are confused about what they are supposed to be doing and feel bad about it.
- They are trying to hide a disability.
- They are trying to hide their lack of a particular skill (reading, math).
- They are being teased, ridiculed, or ostracized by their peers.
- They are unable to ask for help from an adult because they are ashamed, embarrassed, or frightened.
- They feel lonely.
- They feel isolated.
- They feel different.
- They feel no one understands.

An inclusive classroom is designed to make sure children do not have experiences like these at school.

When a child who has exhibited behavior problems in a general education classroom improves just by moving to a more supportive, inclusive one that provides accommodations, appropriate assignments, a collegial atmosphere, and opportunities for success, was the problem with the child or with his school environment? Our goal must be to support all students, understand the meaning behind their behavior, and provide what they need, such as those things in the following list, to help them succeed in every classroom of the school:

- Accommodations and supports that allow them to perform tasks and follow routines
- Work that challenges them at their level
- Daily experiences of academic success
- The feeling that they are an accepted and valued part of the class
- Friendly relationships with peers and teachers
- Extra help building academic skills when necessary

- Accommodations related to specific disabilities
- Curriculum that values and informs children as individuals

Sometimes children may exhibit behavior problems for no apparent reason: they *could* be successful but seem to choose not to. In that case, their home life could be difficult and stressful: divorce, drugs, domestic violence, depression, unemployment, the serious illness or death of a family member, are formidable troubles for anyone. Obviously, we cannot do much to change circumstances like these; however, it is important to acknowledge that these are huge issues in children's lives and have a profound affect on their ability to function in school. We can try to make school, at least, a safe and nurturing place in which these children are able to feel successful and in control. Life has been described as being bittersweet, and while we may not be able to remove the bitter parts, we are able to add some sweetness to each child's life at school every day.

Children (especially young children) may also have a difficult time with events in their home life that grownups view as normal—Dad going away on a business trip, Mom going to the hospital for minor surgery, the arrival of a new baby brother or sister. These things can nevertheless have a big emotional impact and cause children to act in challenging ways. (And an emotional problem can manifest itself in physical symptoms.) Children aren't always aware that not everyone knows what they are experiencing, and even if they wanted to, they may not have the language or the insight to tell us how they feel or why they are doing the things they do.

Again, whatever the specific circumstances, we need to try to provide any support we can. Here are some possibilities:

- Contact the school administration to make sure the child and family are receiving available help.
- Ask the guidance counselor or school psychologist to let the child join a support group of children dealing with similar situations (divorce, sickness, death in the family, etc.).
- Allow the child to come in early or stay late to complete homework.
- Make sure the child has needed materials for projects and assignments that are done at home (poster board, markers, etc.).
- Communicate with family members about issues the child may be facing and problem-solve together.
- Provide a safe, secure environment in which learning, success, and fun are part of each day.
- Understand that weekends may be especially difficult, and this may show up in the child's behavior on Mondays.

Giving a child who is going through a difficult time support, accommodations, and the opportunity to feel successful and valued will bring some immediate improvement, although behavior challenges that were years in the making will not completely disappear overnight. You will see continued improvement over time, as the child begins to trust your ability to make school enjoyable. You may eventually find you enjoy having this child in your class! (And other teachers in your school may ask about your magic formula.)

■ A Powerful New Lens

While supporting positive behavior is not simple, taking a problem-solving approach makes it a lot easier than we thought it could be. This approach is based on several assumptions.

The first assumption is that while we commonly say children *have a behavior problem,* this is inaccurate. Disruptive children *are being challenged by a problem* that most likely exists in the classroom environment, the curriculum, their social relationships, or their home life. The challenging behavior is a *symptom of a problem* that is not necessarily theirs. We need to determine what and where the problem is and take the steps necessary to provide support.

The second assumption is that all children are driven to learn, are curious, and will strive for mastery. When the children in your class were babies, they were naturally motivated to practice for many hours each day to learn to walk and talk. And now they may have the persistence and motivation to work for hours mastering a sport and/or a video game. If you follow an exercise regimen or have read the directions to a video game, you know these endeavors require focus, perseverance, and diligence in order to do well and make progress. Many children who seem unable to do their schoolwork are devoted to these challenging free-time pursuits and find them engaging and enjoyable. We need to take the techniques intrinsic to learning to play games and apply them in our classroom: interacting, getting immediate feedback, experiencing quantifiable progress, making choices, learning from experience, gaining mastery through practice, and having a measure of control of the learning process. The more we can incorporate these techniques into the school day, the more we can help students bring the same motivation and focused effort they exhibit outside school to their schoolwork.

The third assumption is that all children not only want to do well in school but also *are doing as well as they can under the particular circumstances and environment in which they find themselves* (Goleman, 1998). Behavior problems are children's way of telling us that the environment does not support their success, much as a baby's cries let us know he needs something.

When we look at behavior, it is important that we choose the lens that gives us the most power to change the situation. Some ways of looking at events make us powerless before them; others let us devise ways to change them for the better. Realizing that children are doing the best they can in their current environment allows us to eliminate the drama, the charged feeling of thinking they are lazy or expressing their disdain for school. Now, we can move on to solve the problem.

Some children who are able to do very little under the circumstances in which they find themselves at school may be able to do much better, academically and socially, when the circumstances change. This is a powerful concept: while it is impossible to change other people's behavior directly, we do have the ability to affect it by changing the environment and rearranging the circumstances in which they find themselves.

Children's behavior may be related to the environment, the work they are asked to do, or a learning challenge. It may stem from an emotional challenge, a social problem, or a cognitive difference. It could also be the result of something that is happening at home. Or perhaps something about our own teaching style or the classroom environment needs to change.

We need to make sure the following elements are in place in our classrooms:

- Appropriate supports and accommodations, both general and those related to the particular learning disabilities of individual students
- A multilevel and differentiated curriculum comprising appropriate academic tasks every child can complete successfully
- A positive social climate that promotes collegial relationships with other students
- A positive teacher-student relationship
- Appropriate specialized instruction, if needed

An inclusive classroom is the foundation that makes behavior management work.

■ Supporting Positive Behavior in the Inclusive Classroom

All children want to be successful. They want to please their teachers and gain the admiration of their peers. Often, they resort to undesirable behavior when for some reason this does not seem possible. Individual children may have come to this conclusion long before they arrived at your door, but now they are in your class, in what they see as a no-win situation. Their behavior problems stem, at least partly, from believing they have nothing to lose.

The first steps to take are always the same:

- With children, establish classroom rules and make sure they are followed.
- Make sure everyone in the class is safe from teasing or bullying (the child behaving disruptively may be the aggressor but may also be the victim).
- Understand children's disabilities. If no disability has been diagnosed but some of the behavior you see is similar to that associated with a particular type of learning challenge, try using the suggested supports.
- Make sure your body language and facial expressions convey that you accept and like the children as they are (isn't that what everyone wants?) and that you value them as class members. Let them know you are there to help and support them in becoming what they want to be: a successful, accepted part of the classroom community.
- Remember that you are dealing with children who are hurting. (This will make the trying times easier to get through.) As tough as they may seem on the outside, many are only trying to protect a fragile, vulnerable core.

■ Changing Your Spots

If the environmental and curricular supports are in place but problems persist, there are several other areas to consider. One of the first things we should look at is our own interactions with students.

Teaching is a profession with many intangible rewards, one of which is seeing children acquire skills and develop as learners. If we teach at the same grade level each year, the curriculum may change very little, and over time we come to know it and our pedagogy very well. But the children change each year. Because our relationship with them is by definition short term, our tendency is to treat them as the problem rather than change the way we deal with them. It is not easy to change this habit, developed by virtue of hundreds of daily interactions, with twenty or more children, individually and as a group, a hundred and eighty days a year, year after year. We may want to develop more effective ways of responding to the children in our class, but wanting to is only part of the battle: it doesn't automatically change our minute-to-minute reactions.

If we are serious about changing our behavior, we first need to decide what it is we want to change. The best way to do this is by thinking about our most successful interactions and what made them so and also about our least successful interactions and what we might have done differently.

It's likely your most successful interactions are with those children whom you would describe as hard working and respectful, no matter what their ability level. These children are most likely similar to you, so it is easy to relate to them. Is there a certain type of child you have difficulty with? It's worthwhile to think about this and try to figure out who and why. It may be that a new cultural or ethnic group has moved into your area and you have difficulty relating to these children. Children from some cultural groups may seem loud or boisterous, and children from others may seem like they are very passive and always waiting for you to tell them what to do and how to do it. Maybe learning more about their culture, their family values, and their traditions and beliefs will help put their behavior into perspective. Is it hard for you to tolerate the type of child that can't sit still, that never has her materials, that always asks you to repeat what you've just said? A learning disability may be part of the problem, and learning more about what is and is not under the control of children with certain learning disabilities, then looking at this as a situation that can be at least partly remedied with classroom supports may be an area to work on. Maybe you have a hard time with a child who can be sarcastic or who acts like the class clown. Is the behavior disrespectful, or does it feel threatening to your authority in the classroom? Rather than react on the spot, plan in advance how you will deal with the situation. You may decide to allow some leeway for jokes but also decide to have a class discussion about appropriate ways to act in school. Reach out to a child who is difficult for you to deal with. It's easy to ask the child you have a good relationship with how her weekend was, and this is a wonderful thing to do. At the same time, extending yourself more to the challenging child may not be easy at first, but the payback will be great as you begin to understand each other and form a positive and caring relationship. For each of us, some children are harder to deal with than others. None of this is easy, and addressing and dealing with issues surrounding children who are challenging for you to deal with will most certainly take you out of your comfort zone; however, the time and effort we put into improving our interactions with children makes us more effective teachers and better people in the long run (Goleman, 1998).

Changing the way we interact with our students also lets us experience what it's like to learn something new and difficult. The cycle of making mistakes, trying again, taking steps forward, and suffering reversals impresses on us in a very concrete way that mistakes are part of learning and that new skills take time to master. It's important to set attainable goals and recognize and celebrate our progress when we meet them. Everyone's goals will be different. We need to analyze our people skills and consciously try to improve them, practicing at school and at home.

Great teachers develop good relationships with all the students in the class, establish themselves as the leader of a group that has an important mission, and "sell" the curriculum. Their students believe that school is important and that what they are learning is valuable. Great teachers generate excitement for the work at hand and persuade and encourage their students to do their best. They are able to interpret their students' nonverbal communication, as individuals and as a group, and use that information to make their lessons more effective. They are able to generate the belief in each of their students that he or she is a valuable class member. Figure 6.2 lists the types of behavior demonstrated by great teachers. Each of us is good at some of these

---

Figure 6.2 *Qualities of great teachers*

Great Teachers

Are fully present when talking to or working with students, which makes their students feel valued and important.

Are calm and positive, which makes their students see them as leaders.

Keep their sense of humor, which makes school enjoyable and fun.

Teach students to value mistakes as part of the learning process, which gives their classrooms an atmosphere of intellectual inquiry.

Always give children a way to save face, which allows their students to take risks knowing their self-esteem will not be jeopardized.

Look for and find something to like about each child in the class, which helps them form relationships with their students.

Give positive feedback on all progress, even small steps in the right direction, which lets their students be successful every day and instills in them the confidence to continue trying.

We All Sometimes

React in a way we later regret.

Take things personally.

Sweat the small stuff (and some say it is all small stuff).

But Great Teachers

Keep trying to improve and resolve to do better next time.

---

things, but the best teachers keep trying to grow and develop to be good at *all* of them.

Everyone is more compatible with some people than with others. You may have a child in your class who is difficult for you to relate to or hard for you to like, but it is essential that you develop a positive working relationship with every child. Keep these ideas in mind:

- Kids are different from grownups; just because we think something isn't a big deal doesn't mean kids agree. (For example, you might think nothing of wearing an outfit that is a bit out of style, but this may be a major disaster for a girl in your class.)
- Some children are very sensitive, and the offhand remark, spoken without malice or intent to hurt, can devastate. Some of us were very sensitive too once, before we developed a thicker skin. (But did we really develop a thicker skin, or did we just learn to hide our feelings better?)
- Just as an innocuous action repeated again and again can blossom into a great annoyance, repeated "failures" (which is how students may view having to ask for directions to be repeated, an additional explanation, extra help; or never receiving an A) become magnified in students' minds and may cause them to overreact.
- It's probably not about you. Children's actions are about their own experiences in school and the way they see themselves there. Children are playing the game of life along with everyone else on the planet. When things are tough, they do things they think will get them around the board in one piece. They're trying to soften the hurt they feel and make it better.
- Children who make misguided choices that provide short-term relief but make their problems worse in the long run have a lot of adult company. Many adults, who arguably should know better, sometimes think they can handle problems with alcohol, drugs, or other risky behavior.
- Most students' relationship with you will be one of many supportive relationships they have with adults; your relationship with students who have behavior challenges may be one of very few (or even the only one).

■ Moving Toward Support for All

The supports and accommodations of an inclusive classroom usually give diverse learners what they need to be able to succeed; however, they aren't always enough. If a student in your class has a learning disability, the special educator will help you incorporate the proper accommodations into your classroom and will provide the child with specialized instruction. However, it is also important for you to understand the disability, why the accommodations are important, the effect the learning challenges have on the child and those around him, and what he can and cannot control. (The disability profiles in Chapter 2 will help you do this.)

Sometimes a child's disruptive behavior may occur only in school and nowhere else. How the parent sees the child and how the teacher sees the child are then very different. The general education environment is very hard on those who have learning challenges, and interfering behavior may not be totally under the child's control. If you suspect a child has an undocumented disability or is not receiving appropriate services, bring it up with the special educator and your colleagues. (This is discussed more fully in Chapters 8 and 9 on building an educational team and working with the special educator.)

Think about the top student in your class and the one showing the most behavior problems, and analyze the differences in their experiences during the day. Then think about how you can narrow the distance between their experiences—how you can decrease the challenged student's failures and increase her successes and positive interactions. While many of the accommodations and curricular adjustments of the inclusive classroom are powerful ways to effect positive changes for a student like this, if there is a learning challenge as well, or if the child is significantly behind in reading, writing, or math, specialized instruction is necessary. This is undertaken based on a plan prepared in conjunction with the special educator and other members of your educational team.

The following behavior problems may stem from a learning challenge:

- Habitual tardiness
- Forgetting homework, books, and materials at home
- Coming to class without the required materials
- Not following directions
- Answering questions without waiting to be called on
- Not completing assignments
- Not remembering what was taught
- Not doing homework
- Not understanding what was said
- Appearing not to pay attention during lessons
- Fiddling or playing with objects during lessons
- Doodling during lessons

The following behavior problems may stem from not having the required skills or being asked to complete tasks that are too difficult:

- Claiming to not understand what was said
- Being the class clown
- Appearing not to pay attention during lessons
- Not doing homework
- Dashing off assignments, doing the least amount of work possible
- Talking to a classmate during a lesson

If the majority of the class is exhibiting this behavior, however, it may be an indication that the class work is not engaging the students sufficiently. Adding more hands-on experiences, opportunities to work in groups, and opportunities to make choices may be what is needed.

■ Giving Disruptive Behavior a Face

Robert is a fourth grader who you hypothesize is behaving disruptively because his reading skills are significantly below grade level. (Perhaps one reason it has taken this long to pinpoint the problem is that Robert has very successfully diverted attention from his reading challenges to his behavior.) He has learned to read a large number of words by sight but has not yet internalized the sound-symbol correspondence of language, which makes it hard for him to decode new or unfamiliar words. He avoids reading in general and doesn't read for pleasure, which only adds to his difficulties.

Several things are going on here:

- Reading is an essential and integral skill. If Robert cannot decode and/or understand what he is reading, he will fall behind in every subject. Many children are so ashamed of not being able to read the material assigned that they cannot ask for help; instead, they hide their problem by misbehaving.
- Behavior is communicative. What Robert is trying to tell you, and probably has been trying to tell his former teachers, year after year, is that he can't read, and he is ashamed and worried about it. As he has fallen further and further behind, his misbehavior has escalated. He's been screaming at his teachers, *I can't do this*, while his teachers, not understanding, shake their heads and wonder why he can't get hold of himself and buckle down to work. It's a sad dance.
- Paradoxical as it seems, Robert cares very much about school and about being viewed as being as capable as the other students in his

class. The evidence is the trouble he has gone to in order to hide his disability, even at the cost of getting the help he needs.

- His disruptive behavior may have caused him to be out of the room a lot and certainly keeps him from attending to lessons, which impedes his progress even more.
- Year after year Robert has read fewer books than his peers, so he has less knowledge to draw from to make sense of new information and connect with it. He probably also has a weaker vocabulary than his peers.
- His self-esteem is very fragile, and he is unable to admit his handicap. Even though he knows he needs help in this no-win situation, he may not be able to ask for or accept it.
- He will not easily tolerate doing work that he views as being easier or different from the work the rest of the class is doing.

Robert needs two types of academic help: (1) general classroom scaffolds and modifications, and (2) direct instruction and appropriate practice to increase his reading skills—but first the misbehavior impeding his progress needs to be reduced. The behavior is there for a purpose—to protect him from having to admit to himself or anyone else that he has a reading problem. It's a bandage protecting a wound. As long as the wound is open, it needs the bandage to cover and protect it, but as the body forms its own protective scab, the bandage can be removed. (If it's a very bad wound, there may always be a scar.)

The first step is to change the bandage (behavior) for a different one that is going to help the wound heal. The new bandage still has to protect (and cover up) the wound but should also promote progress. It also needs to be applied gently but matter-of-factly *(of course this is what we are going to do)*, without pity or blame.

Let's get specific. During reading workshop, while the other students are reading independently or writing their reader response letter, Robert spends his time staring at a book that is far above his reading level, looking at pictures in magazines, trying to distract his tablemates by starting a conversation (he can always find someone willing to go along), writing a reader response letter that is either one sentence long or full of irrelevant remarks he thinks are funny. He wastes the whole period, and you repeatedly have to leave the small group or individual you were working with to redirect him.

Robert needs to read books at his independent reading level, but those books are obviously for younger children and don't interest him. You need an acceptable reason for giving him work that is different from the rest of the class. (It just has to be plausible, not bulletproof.) You decide to ask him for help:

- "I just got some new books on tape that I need to listen to and write sample reader responses for, but I don't have the time. Could you do it for me?"
- "I am thinking of using these short stories with a student in a different class. Can you try them out for me and tell me what you think?"
- "I'm starting a book group and would love to have you in it, because I think you would really enjoy the book we're going to read. But I only have three copies—would you mind listening to the book on tape instead?"
- "There is a first grader who is having a hard time with reading. I wonder if you could be his reading buddy and read a book to him once a week?"

By applying bandages like these, you help him build his academic and background knowledge and vocabulary; read independently; and think, discuss, and write about the books and stories he reads. At first, you make sure the work is at or even slightly below a level he can accomplish successfully and give him ample positive feedback. As his confidence in his ability to progress grows, he begins to trust you.

When the wound has healed a bit, you mention that some kids have trouble with reading and that reading is not easy. You explain that the best way to get better is to read books that are at just the right level and show him the area in the classroom library where he can choose these kinds of books. You also let him know that if there are other books he wants to read that are too hard at the moment, he can listen to them on tape. You further explain that you help a lot of kids build reading strategies for figuring out what to do when they come to a word they don't understand and that you and he will work on this together.

The point to keep in mind is this: the behavior is serving a purpose. If you can serve that purpose in a way that allows a child to learn and progress, you will be able to provide the daily success and feelings of accomplishment that are essential to the learning experience. The child's behavioral challenges will decrease accordingly.

■ The Exception to the Rule

There is one instance where you *can* change other people's behavior directly, when telling them how they should act and setting up a behavior plan may be the best and most efficient thing to do. What appears to be undesirable behavior in children on the autism spectrum (symptoms may vary from mild to severe) is often a case of misinterpreting social cues or not knowing what to do or how to act in school or in social situations. In this case, directly teaching what the acceptable behavior is, why this behavior is preferred, and how the undesirable behavior affects others will help the children adapt. It also helps to warn children of the autism spectrum about new situations and tells them in advance how to act (Gray, 2000).

To help you understand how direct teaching helps children with these challenges, imagine that you receive an invitation to an inaugural ball at the White House. You've never attended one before and have many questions about what to do and how to act. What should you wear? Which door should you enter? Where should you stand? What should you say when you met the new president and first lady? When is it okay to chat with those at your table, and when should you be quiet? You'll feel very relieved if someone simply tells you the answers. It would also be great to know the names (and even better, have pictures) of those who'll be sitting near you and be told something about them that will make it easier to start a conversation. Knowing this information, your anxiety will be greatly reduced, and you might even be able to enjoy yourself.

An inaugural ball is only a few hours on a single night. School is five days a week, ten months a year. Some children on the autism spectrum like having a way to self monitor their behavior. Checklists or cards that remind them what to do and/or how to act are often welcome, as they can effectively support their efforts.

In Summary

Setting up a classroom that supports everyone is not only the most effective way to teach all of the children in your class, it is also an effective way to prevent interfering behavior.

Human behavior is communicative. When we unravel what children are trying to tell us with their behavior, we are able to make changes that will result in a better school experience and improved behavior.

Undesirable behavior is a symptom of a problem at school or at home. We must take steps to determine what the problem is and provide the supports we can to the environment, in the curriculum, and in interpersonal relationships.

It's important that we continuously work on our people skills in our interactions with our students and consciously try to improve them.

Knowledge of disabilities helps us implement accommodations and understand their purpose and importance.

Direct teaching of social skills and using behavior plans is a welcome and effective intervention for children on the autism spectrum.

7 | Inclusive Classroom Assessment

I n every classroom, including inclusion classrooms, we are continuously assessing our students. We do this during conferences when we are talking with them about their work and their thinking and as we walk around the classroom observing them and listening to them while they work with peers in small groups. We do it when we look at children's individual work and as we listen to their contributions to whole-class discussions. We assess their end-of-unit projects, listen to their presentations, and watch their performances; and in the process, we develop a true understanding of what they can do and how they are progressing. These assessments also help us see what we need to do to move them forward.

Another important form of assessment in all classrooms is student self-assessment that allows children to see and appreciate their own growth over time. At the end of a unit, or periodically throughout the year, when we ask children to spend some time going through their work folders to choose pieces of work for their portfolios with a written reflection about why they chose that particular example, the children learn about themselves as learners, and we learn about them too. This is also a perfect time to ask them to set a goal for themselves to work toward over the coming weeks and months. Building a portfolio allows each child to decide what is important to him or her, assigning importance to a piece by choosing it for the portfolio. A child's reflection on why he included one piece of work may reveal he chose it because the process he went through to create or construct it was an important learning experience for him, and a reflection for another piece may state that he is proud of what he produced.

Another necessary assessment tool is the rubric. We provide our students with rubrics to give them another way to monitor and evaluate their own quality of work, to make the grades they receive understandable and the path to doing better next time clear. Through all of these classroom assessments, we come to know our students as individual learners, each with his or her set of strengths and weaknesses. We get a picture of each child that is both broad and deep and that provides the information we need to move them forward and stretch their thinking. These assessments are the basis of how we accurately come to know and understand each of our students' growth and progress throughout the year.

It is also important to have an idea of the general strengths and weaknesses of the class as a whole right from the start of the year. One of the best ways to get a whole-class overview, as well as the relative abilities of the individual students in it, is to conduct skill assessments at the beginning of the year that can also serve as benchmarks for evaluating future progress. These benchmark assessments are valuable tools for determining whether any students need additional support. As the year goes on, they can be used to determine the effectiveness of particular strategies or approaches.

Assessments should be administered to all students at the beginning, middle, and end of the year. The beginning-of-the-year assessments help us understand as much as possible about the students' current level of achievement and uncover areas in which individual students need help. In the middle of the year, assessments let us know whether students are making satisfactory progress or not. The end-of-the-year assessments provide information we need to make placement recommendations for next year.

During the initial weeks of school, administer the following set of assessments:

- Writing to a prompt (hopefully, something more engaging than the classic "write about something you did on your summer vacation"). For younger children, we might dictate a list of words for them to spell in order to ascertain their level of phonemic awareness, or ask them to draw a picture and write a sentence or label underneath.

- A reading inventory, administered individually. This assesses a child's decoding and word-attack strategies, fluency and expression, and ability to retell or summarize the story. Depending on grade level, it may also assess inferential comprehension.

- An inventory of basic math skills. Depending on grade level, the inventory may assess the ability to add, subtract, multiply, and divide; knowledge of place value, fractions, decimals, and percents; the ability to solve a word problem; and the ability to solve problems in more than one way.

Remember, we are looking for information about the strengths and weaknesses of each student as well as the strengths and weaknesses of the class as a whole. A third-grade teacher I know scores all her reading inventories together. She enters the salient information on each child's record but does not assign a score until all the inventories have been completed. Then she calculates the final scores and creates a continuum showing the range of skills in the class and which students are average, high, or low in relation to their peers (as well as any outliers). This is a good method to use with the writing and math assessments as well.

The beginning-of-the-year assessments are a useful way to identify whole-class needs and plan instructional steps to meet those needs. For example, after reviewing the results of the math assessments, we may decide to start the daily math period with five minutes of mental math or display a word problem on the board for the students to solve, then spend a few minutes sharing answers and strategies. Or we may decide to start each writing workshop by having the students edit a sentence and go over it as a group. The reading assessment provides information that enables us to have books on hand at the independent reading level of everyone in the class, especially those children who are reading below grade level.

Looking at the results on a continuum lets us identify students who may need extra help in math, reading, and/or writing, as well as those who may benefit from curricular extensions. We will also have specific information right from the start to share with the special educator, so together we can effectively support students with IEPs as well as others facing learning challenges.

In order to make sure the interventions put in place in September are effective, it's a good idea to retest students again in the middle of the year, preferably the entire class but certainly the students about whom we are concerned. As we all know, not every plan or strategy works the way we hoped or intended, so a second benchmark in the middle of the year informs our plans for supporting children who are in danger of falling behind. If a student is making progress as a result of the interventions currently in place, we can continue to use them. If a student's progress is not satisfactory, we know we'll need to work with the team to try different approaches when we plan the second half of the year.

A final assessment is given at the end of the year. These assessments provide helpful information for making placement decisions and serve as useful tools as we reflect on the year just past and plan for next year: what worked well, what didn't work as well, and which adjustments were successful.

■ Embedded Assessments

In inclusive classrooms, as in general education classrooms, we continuously assess students' understanding. Each day we listen and observe as students participate in class discussions, work together as a class and in small groups, explain their thinking, share their work, and talk about their ideas. Many teachers make notes in a log, on post-it notes, or on a class roster as they walk around and observe. These assessments give us the most and the best quality information about our students.

Many imbedded classroom assessments have a dual purpose: gauging students' skills while at the same time helping them expand their thinking or skills and move forward. These assessments work well for typical learners as well as those with diverse learning styles. One such assessment is the writing workshop conference, a one-on-one discussion of students' writing in which teacher and child review the piece under development and decide how to make the writing better. This assessment is especially clear and helpful if it is based on a rubric (Calkins, 2006, pp. 106–107; see also each *Unit of Study*).

Another form of evaluation is the reader response journal, in which we assess students' reading comprehension, ask questions that make the students think more deeply about what they have read, and suggest other books or genres that will increase the depth of their thinking and the breadth of their reading. We can also assess children's reading comprehension by listening to book discussion groups or talking with students about the books they are reading (Fountas and Pinnell, 2001). In math, having children explain their thinking about how they solved a problem is a way to assess children's work and for the other children in the class to hear about other ways to solve a problem (Fosnot and Dolk, 2001). These assessments also reveal whether certain concepts are difficult for the whole class or only a few and help us plan accordingly.

■ Traditional Assessments

Many diverse learners have difficulty with the more traditional written assessments, such as standardized multiple choice exams, end-of-unit essay and short-answer tests, pop quizzes, and long-term projects, and they may need accommodations or scaffolds in order to be able to show what they know.

Traditional assessments are a part of school life, so it is important to be sure the tests are fair and give an accurate indication of what students know. When children with diverse needs and/or learning challenges take such formal tests, accommodations like the following are often necessary:

- Schedule frequent breaks.
- Administer the test at a time of day dictated by students' medical or learning needs.
- Administer the test to a small group.
- Administer the test in a location other than the classroom, such as a small office or conference room for children who need a distraction-free environment or who need extra time and would feel pressured to stop working as other children turn in their work.
- Administer the test in a specific part of the classroom (the front row, a study carrel or other enclosed area to limit distractions).
- Provide noise buffers.
- Read the test aloud and/or clarify test directions.
- Have a familiar person administer the test.
- Let students use magnifying equipment or enlarging or amplifying devices.
- Allow students to use colored visual overlays.
- Permit students to use a large-print version of the test.
- Let students use a Braille version of the test.
- Allow students to use a place marker.
- Guide the student from one question to the next so that none are accidentally missed.
- Redirect students' attention to the test.
- Read individual test questions aloud (excluding reading passages on a language, literature or reading test).
- Sign test questions for students who are deaf or hard of hearing.
- Permit students to use an electronic text reader (except language, literature and reading tests).
- Have students dictate responses to a scribe.
- Let students use a graphic organizer, checklist, refer to a mathematics reference sheet or notebook, or use an abacus or number line.

These accommodations don't change the test, only the way information is given or received or the environment in which the test is taken.

When a student has an IEP, the accommodations for testing are specified; however, other diverse learners may benefit from them as well. Some accommodations help students understand what is being asked; for example, a student reading below grade level may need to have a math word problem read aloud. Some students may lose their place and require a place marker. A student with poor vision may need a large-print version of the test. Other accommodations help students provide their answers. For example, students for whom the physical act of writing is difficult may give very short responses unless they are allowed to answer orally or use a keyboard. Still other accommodations are related to the test environment. Some children do much better if they are tested in a space separate from the rest of the class, are given extra time to complete the test, or are allowed to take breaks during the test.

When we give an assessment and grade an individual's work, we find out how well that student understands the subject matter. If most students in the class get a certain question wrong or have difficulty with a certain concept, we find something out about the way we have structured the lessons and learning experiences around the concept, and we may discover that the class needs more experience or practice with the concept or skill. Test results are an additional tool to help us understand what the individuals in our classes know and to determine our next instructional steps. If mastery is essential, based on district learning goals, we won't move on until most of the class has achieved it, and we'll provide extra support for the few students who haven't. If a concept will be revisited, we may note those who had difficulty but move on, knowing there will be additional opportunities for reteaching and practice. However, we must be careful not to use this as a justification for not putting in extra support; without that support, the same few individuals may fall further behind each time the concept is taught.

Assessing is not the same as teaching, and it does not help children learn. If all we do is give a timed test of multiplication facts at the beginning of every math class, we will be disappointed to find that the children aren't doing any better this week than they did two weeks ago. Children need daily mini-lessons and daily practice, not daily tests. Traditional assessments on their own do not increase skills. The best assessments are imbedded in the daily work of learning; they are part of the learning process, either because they expand students' thinking or because they are designed to reinforce what the students are learning while giving us the opportunity to observe and interact with students as they work. Imbedded classroom assessments give us a clearer idea of students' thinking, understanding, and misunderstanding, and give us an authentic way to help them understand the material better.

Diverse learners are often not good test takers, and describing their achievement level by how well they do on a traditional written assessment may not be fair. Those who once do badly on a test even though they have studied for it may become tense or be unable to recall the material on all future tests. Some children have memory challenges that make learning and regurgitating a large number of facts close to impossible. We need assessment tools that tell us what we need to know and that work with all students. You might try the following strategies:

- Avoid using one or two comprehensive assessments that test large amounts of material. Frequent assessments, by checking homework or even a short daily quiz on the current material, are much better: The students are studying smaller, more manageable chunks of information, and they know each grade is worth only a small percentage of their final grade. They are not under as much pressure, and we can spot and remediate misunderstandings of the material before they are compounded.
- When we do give an end-of-unit assessment or any other longer, more comprehensive test, we should prepare a study guide. A week or several days before the test, we can distribute the guide and go over it with the whole class. This allows students time to ask for clarification and to study the material.
- Scaffold long-term projects: establish intermediate due dates to help children plan their time, provide organizers to help them take notes, give specific and detailed descriptions of what they are required to do, set aside times when they can consult us if they run into problems.
- Don't purposely try to stump the students by not telling them what material a test will cover or by putting in trick questions.
- When assessing understanding and knowledge in a content area (particularly in the higher grades), let students use the notes they've taken in class and during their reading. Taking and using notes is a life skill. Adults frequently look things up or refer to their notes at work. Allowing students to do this encourages them to take good notes and keep them organized over the course of the unit.
- If possible, try to use a familiar test format.

Using accommodations and gathering assessment information in many different ways is best and gives us more accurate and complete information about our students' understanding of the material being taught.

■ About Grading

Grading is used for many things, and in the upper grades is unavoidable, but what it does not do is help children learn or progress. In an inclusion classroom where there are many children working at different levels, we need to be careful and use the motivational aspect grades can have to encourage students to try harder or try again. The following lists some traditional ways to use grades:

- Sort and rank students.
- Assign a grade, letter, or number to their skills or understanding.
- Motivate students to work harder, to get a good grade.
- Give students feedback about the quality of their work.
- Obtain information that tells teachers when to move on to the next unit.
- For adults, a certain grade on a qualifying exam may be needed to get into college (SAT or ACT), get a driver's license, become a teacher, doctor, or lawyer, among other occupations.

Multiple-choice tests and other tests looking for factual answers are graded based on correct and incorrect responses. Other types of assessments can be subjective to grade and so are most fair when the standard or rubric used to judge the work is explicit and available. There are many ready-made rubrics on the Internet, as well as procedures for developing a rubric specific to a particular purpose. When work is graded using a rubric, students can clearly see what was expected in order to obtain a certain grade and what actions or skills would have earned them a higher score. This is valuable feedback. It also keeps the grader objective, because the work is being evaluated against a set of explicit criteria.

If we and/or the special educator modify class work (fewer or less difficult problems to solve, simpler books to read, a less stringent rubric or standard), assessments need to be modified accordingly. This brings up the problem of how to clearly communicate the status of two children, both with A averages, one who is doing modified assignments and one who is not. They are both doing high quality work, but their achievement level is not the same. How do we communicate on the report card of the child with the modified curriculum that she is working hard, learning, and making progress at her own level, but is not doing grade-level work? One way is to give the earned grade followed by an asterisk (A*) linked to a statement that the child is being graded on her progress toward the goals stated in her IEP rather than district goals for the grade level. This gives her credit for her work and accurately represents her achievement level.

■ Retaking Tests

If and when you must give a formal test, the best ones cover small chunks of material at a time, and this approach is good practice for all learners. It takes a great deal of the drama and stress out of test taking, since each assessment is only a small part of the final grade; it gives us frequent feedback on what to review with some or all of the class; and it helps children practice taking tests and become more comfortable in the testing environment. If we are using the assessment primarily to see what children know, along with a secondary goal of motivating the child to exert effort, allowing children to study more and have an option to retake a test in order to improve their grade is a good strategy. Some teachers give everyone in the class the opportunity to review the items they answered incorrectly and redo those items, either on a separate piece of paper or on the same paper in a different-color ink or pencil, to earn a higher grade. Other teachers offer a time several days later when students who did not do as well as they wished can take the test again. This prompts children to study more and have that extra effort reflected in their grade and gives them a sense that they have some control over how well they do. This is not a special accommodation; it is something granted to adults in the real world without any negative repercussions. For example, if the licensing boards for lawyers, doctors, and teachers did not allow those hoping to enter these fields the opportunity to retake qualifying exams, there would be far fewer practitioners at work today. If someone is willing to put in the effort to study and learn the material, their accomplishment should be granted the same reward even if it takes them extra time and another try.

In Summary

The best assessments are observations, conferences, portfolios projects, performances, and presentations that are imbedded in our teaching and allow us to assess and move a child forward at the same time.

Assessments at the beginning of the year provide valuable information on the class as a whole and on individuals within the class.

Reassessing them at the year's midpoint is an opportunity to determine whether children (especially those about whom we are concerned) are progressing and, if not, make a better plan.

Accommodations are sometimes necessary in order to get a true picture of what some children know. We may need to change the environment in which the test is given or the way a child is asked the questions or responds to them.

If you decide to use traditional assessments:

- Assess frequently through checking homework or short daily quizzes that focus on small chunks of information.
- Provide necessary accommodations.
- Try to use a standard format.
- Provide study guides for unit tests.
- Don't ask trick questions.
- Allow students to consult their notes during the test if good note taking is one of the things being taught.
- Reward effort: allow students to do extra work, study more, and retake assessments in order to improve their grade.

8 | Communicating and Collaborating with Parents

T eachers communicate with parents in various ways—a welcome letter at the beginning of the year, a weekly or monthly newsletter about what is going on in the classroom, parent night conferences, and contact by telephone or e-mail. Some teachers send home a postcard with "good news" about each child in the class a few times a year. When we have children with IEPs in our classroom, we want those parents to be part of the special education team. Parents of children with learning challenges may be more anxious than other parents, and this anxiety may increase each year. We need to recognize this concern and address it.

When my older daughter was in third grade, we moved to a new town. Her teacher the year before was very traditional, good in many ways, but my daughter often came home with hurt feelings over things that I as an adult could see the teacher was unaware of and hadn't meant negatively. But no matter how I tried to explain it, it didn't make things easier for my daughter, who told me, "I'm learning a lot, but it's not very pleasant." When we went to meet her teacher in our new town, I knew my prayers had been answered. She was amazingly kind and wonderful; her classroom was a happy mélange of plants, critters, work on display, and work in progress. She welcomed my daughter warmly and talked with her in a way that let me know she was in good hands.

Still, the next year I was apprehensive about sending my younger daughter to kindergarten in this new place and hoped she would get a good teacher as well. I don't remember much about that kindergarten year (uneventful, no major problems), but I do remember very clearly the short speech the (very wise) principal gave to the parents of incoming kindergarteners. He said he knew how precious our children were, that he understood we were handing them over to strangers and how hard that is to do. He said he knew we were wondering whether the teachers would be kind, whether they would understand our children's quirks, and whether they really understood how absolutely astonishingly amazing each and every one of them was. He then said they did know and that they would nurture the children, guide them, and make learning enjoyable and fun. He said all this sincerely, no kidding around. By the end of his speech, he had the formerly anxious parents, me among them, feeling relieved and laughing sheepishly at having their inner thoughts revealed. He had said what we all needed and wanted to hear.

Years later, when I sent my daughters off to college, I would have been comforted if a similar speech had been given by the head of the college to the parents of freshmen. It would have made things much easier.

■ Fostering Collaboration

In order to enlist parents of diverse learners as part of a special education team, it's important that they see us as people who know their children and understand their learning challenges or disabilities. These parents are well aware that their children have challenges; what they want to know is how we and the rest of the team will support these children. Some teams ask parents about any concerns they have in the phone call confirming the annual meeting. Others ask parents to send in their concerns in writing. Either way, the team then has a chance to think about the concerns and decide how to address them, and the parents feel they have a voice in what goes on. It's important that parents feel heard and that their concerns are addressed.

Parents want to be sure we know their children as people, not just a set of challenges, so we shouldn't save positive information for the end of the meeting but rather begin by reporting a success: academic progress; triumph in a situation that has traditionally been difficult, either academically, socially, or behaviorally; a time the child exerted effort or other positive behavior. Parents also want to know we like their children and can see their strengths and good personal qualities, and relating positive information lets them know we do. A good home-school connection is crucial. We all need to be working for the same purpose—what is best for the children—and we all need to be on the same side.

When parents listen to a laundry list of what sounds to them like complaints—"He is always late, his homework is never done, he talks when he should be working, he doesn't put in the effort, he needs to try harder"—they may feel as if they need to defend their child. Even if everything on the list is true, each item should be discussed separately, and those discussions should include how we as a team have been working to find out why it is happening and explain how we are helping the child change the behavior, be more successful academically, or become better organized. We should also ask parents whether they encounter similar behavior at home and inquire how they handle it. Together we can then develop and implement a successful home-school plan.

Parents' views of, feelings about, and hopes for their children are very important. Some parents see that their children are working hard and making progress and support them and celebrate their progress. Other parents, whose children are also working hard and making the same progress, may not be happy with it or with them. Still other parents may not want their children to be held to normal standards, such as doing their homework or independent reading, believing it is too difficult. In these and similar situations it's important that parents are given time to express their views and their vision before the other members of the team explain their views and their vision and the reasoning behind them. If the meeting is being held to develop IEP goals, the viewpoints of all team members should be taken into consideration—including the parents—and goals that represent high but achievable expectations need to be developed. The goals will need to satisfy everyone on the team if collaboration is to take place.

When parents are unhappy with their children's progress, adding more special education support, scheduling extra time with the teacher or the special educator during the day or before school, and sending home additional work may be in order. If parents feel their children are being given too much homework, perhaps limiting the time spent on homework to a half hour each day (or some other appropriate time frame) will be an acceptable compromise. Children who face organizational issues can be supplied with and supported in using assignment books and checklists, and those with behavioral or social problems can be part of an organized lunch bunch or other forum where they can practice new ways of interacting.

Encouraging parents to phone or e-mail the teacher, the special educator, or any other member of the team whenever they need to also promotes collaboration and keeps everyone apprised of any issues or changes that could affect children at school.

■ Reaching Out to Parents

Some parents may come to a meeting, agree with everything that is said, but offer no input of their own. This is not a good thing. The team needs parents' wants and ideas to make the best possible plan for their children. Sometimes the reason for their reticence is cultural; the family may come from a background in which teachers were never questioned. Other times the parents may see teachers as the experts and simply go along. These parents need encouraging to become part of the process, and any misunderstandings and/or dissatisfaction should be discussed and resolved.

Other parents may seem uninterested in participating in team meetings when in fact they are unable to—they are working, they do not have child care, they do not have transportation, or they are having some other difficulty. If that's the case, we can send out meeting notices several weeks before the meeting date to give parents time to make arrangements; we can offer to schedule the meeting in the early morning or on a day or time that is convenient; we can arrange for someone to watch younger siblings during the meeting, or we can provide a ride to and from school. If the parents are not fluent in English, we need to arrange for a translator and provide all notices and forms in their native language.

It's important to remember that all parents love their children and try to do the best for them they can. Families may be going through hard times, and some parents may not have the resources, either financial or emotional, to do more than they are doing, but hardly ever will we encounter parents who just don't care. Parents know their children better than anyone and need to be encouraged to ask questions and present their concerns and vision for their children. This results in a better plan for the children, more home-school collaboration, and fewer problems down the road.

When we communicate with parents, we must be welcoming, both in our words and in our body language. At the start of a meeting, we need to introduce everyone and make sure the parents know the title and function of anyone they haven't met before. During the meeting, especially when the parents are talking, we must make sure our demeanor says we are listening and open to hearing what they have to say—we should lean forward, maintain eye contact, smile slightly, and nod to show we agree with or at least understand what they are saying. We should pay attention to parents' body language as well. If parents are verbally agreeing but their body language communicates something else, we should ask some open-ended questions to try to get them to express their concerns (see Goleman, 1998).

Another way we can support parents, especially those with children who are being given an IEP for the first time, is to take time to explain the reports and test results and provide materials or sources for finding out more about the children's challenges. Copying the appropriate disability profile from this book (see Chapter 2) and giving it to parents is a starting point. Many parents may want information on how to help their children at home, what to expect, and how to support the efforts of the teachers and their children at school. Providing this information, or telling parents where to find it, is an essential service.

■ Reporting Progress

Many teachers send home a card or a note to acknowledge good work or effort. This is a good practice that rewards the children and builds a stronger relationship between teachers and parents. E-mail is another way to let parents know about children's progress and challenges. This is especially important if there seems to be a "disconnect" between home and school. Perhaps the parents don't realize their daughter begins each day upset because she did her homework but left it at home. Asking parents to help this girl make sure her homework is in her backpack the night before can save a great deal of stress. A "Good news!" phone call or "How's it going?" e-mail is also welcome to parents.

In all grades, but particularly in middle school and above, it is important to let parents know children are failing a subject well in advance so that a plan to turn the situation around can be mutually devised. Parents who think everything is fine and then are handed a report card with poor grades are, understandably, going to be upset. In addition to report cards, parents of children on IEPs receive progress notes from the special educator and any other specialists working with their child. These reports convey children's progress toward their goals, state whether that progress is sufficient for the goals to be met by the end of the IEP period, and, if not, enumerate the instructional changes that will help the children make the necessary progress. Sometimes a child may receive a positive report from the special educator and a much less positive one from the classroom teacher or vice versa. This reflects the different goals, environments, and tasks being evaluated by each teacher.

When parents become upset or angry, we need to stay calm and listen to what they have to say without interrupting. We can use the same positive body language described earlier and remain open to the fact that they may have a legitimate complaint. Sometimes, too, the stress of having children with learning challenges just needs an outlet. Whatever the case, we need to listen closely to what is being said—it's a good idea to write down the issues parents are concerned about and repeat them to be sure we understand them. This also lets parents know they are being heard. If possible, try to make a plan to deal with the issues right then, while everyone is together. If they can't be dealt with then, everyone will need to meet again after they've had time to look into the situation and come up with some suggestions about how to handle the concerns. We need to imagine how parents feel, how we would feel, and how we would want to be treated if it were our child in this situation. We must show parents that we are willing to work together to resolve the problem in a way everyone finds satisfactory.

As we work toward resolving the problem, it's essential to let the other team members know what has happened, and it's a good idea to let the principal know as well. If parents ask for something we don't have the power to do, such as make an exception to school or district rules, we need to offer to look into it for them or to put them in touch with the person who *can* help them. This will offer them a viable course of action and take the edge off their feelings of frustration. Whenever parents are upset, we need to continue to keep the lines of communication open—even and especially when their reactions are hard to deal with. We are building trust, so we need to do what we say we will and keep parents informed of progress and developments.

In Summary

The following list outlines the basis for a collaborative relationship between parents and a special education team:

- Listen to parents' concerns and vision for their children.
- Communicate how children are doing. Positive communication builds the relationship, and early warnings about insufficient progress and plans to deal with it benefit everyone, especially the children.
- Demonstrate that we know children as people and understand their capabilities, that we don't see them only in terms of their learning challenges. Talk to the parents about children's strengths as well as weaknesses.
- Remember, all parents love their children. If parents do not seem interested in attending meetings or supporting children at home, we need to offer whatever supports we can that will allow them to do so.
- When dealing with upset parents, listen to their concerns with an open mind and work to address those concerns. Make sure we understand the issue and work together to address it. Inform the rest of the team and the principal so no one will be taken by surprise.

Building Your Special Education Team

9

An essential element of an effective inclusion classroom is the special education team supporting students with diagnosed learning disabilities. The team can also help you help children who do not have IEPs but require support or accommodations because of other learning challenges or diverse learning styles. Team members' roles are based on their experience and expertise, but any member of the team can be a catalyst for change. If we are not satisfied with our existing team, we can present our ideas and suggestions for making it more useful and supportive rather than wait to be handed a plan of action that we may not be comfortable with and/or that may not work.

Some teachers get excellent support from their school's special educators; others get far less than they need. For most of us, the reality probably lies somewhere between these extremes. Some of this may have to do with the IEP that dictates the amount of time a special educator spends working with the students in your class and the time he needs to pull children out for specialized instruction; however, pullout time should be limited to specialized instruction that cannot be delivered in the classroom. Nevertheless, there are many things we can do as inclusion teachers to help ourselves while at the same time making our working relationship with special educators more productive. When we move toward inclusive practices, we are being leaders. By making changes that increase our effectiveness with diverse learners, we are setting an example and blazing a trail that our fellow team members will notice and follow. Using inclusive practices also helps us with the last piece of the puzzle, using the special educators and others on the team to get the most support possible for the children in the class. The inclusive structure we have built will support the special educator's efforts as well, making all of the teaching and learning that occurs in our classrooms more effective.

The core members of the team are the classroom teacher, the special educator, and the child's parents. Other members may include a speech and language pathologist, a physical therapist, an occupational therapist, the school guidance counselor or psychologist, and any involved aides or paraprofessionals. The child also becomes a formal team member as she gets older. While the child's classmates are not part of the formal team, their perspective should be considered, since social acceptance is a critical ingredient for success.

With so many people involved, communication is a key part of the process, beginning with a common understanding of the challenges faced by both the child and the teacher. The most effective special education teams have a collegial relationship, are working toward the same goals, and communicate effectively. Some teams form collegial relationships quickly, others require a bit more time, but a huge barrier to doing so can be created when everyone is working toward a different goal or fails to understand that the IEP goal and the classroom goal in reading, for example, is the same overall goal with more than one teacher using their expertise to help the child reach it. All team members must understand what the others are doing and respect the others' work while trying to support each other.

If the classroom teacher is using inclusive instructional methods and the special educator always pulls the child out of class, things are bound to get tense unless an effort is made to understand why: is the special educator uncomfortable with the inclusion model and feels all children on IEPs need to be educated separately, or is she providing specialized instruction to remediate a gap in the child's skills that cannot be delivered in the classroom? Once these questions are answered, you are on your way to working toward better collaboration.

Alternately, if the special educator is trying to work with the child in the classroom—scaffolding and modifying the work—and the classroom teacher continuously suggests that the child be taught a less-difficult curriculum in a separate setting, the teachers need to talk and work on understanding the reasons behind each other's point of view. In this situation the special educator may want to suggest some global accommodations that would make in-class support go more smoothly both during the times when there is a special educator or another adult in the class and when the teacher is in the classroom alone. These accommodations should begin to move the teacher toward building an inclusive environment supportive of both the teacher and the students.

One way to build communication and common understanding would be for team members to study the diverse learner summaries in Chapter 2 of this book. These summaries present functional descriptions of a number of disabilities, recommend specific accommodations, and discuss the kinds of support that teachers, special educators, parents, and classmates may provide.

Successful teams and collaborations often take time to develop. The participants must understand one another's points of view, pressures, and needs. Some of these differences are byproducts of the team members' different roles. The classroom teacher, special educator, school psychologist or guidance counselor, speech and language pathologist, occupational therapist, and the physical therapist all have goals from the district and the IEP, and the forum in which these goals must be addressed and met is the classroom. This takes understanding and coordination, with team members getting together to devise a balanced, practical-to-carry-out plan that supports every child in attaining his goals. In any classroom with a child on an IEP, collaboration is key to a year that is successful academically and in every other way. In an inclusive classroom it is just a bit easier.

There are several things we as classroom teachers can do to facilitate collaboration with the special educator and the special education team:

- Communicate regularly. Everyone is busy, but weekly meetings with the special educator (and other team members if appropriate), along with interim e-mails, are essential.
- Realize that the diverse learners in the class are a shared responsibility. Instruction by the special educator is a continuation of classroom instruction and related to it.
- Understand that teams may take time to develop, but sharing information, expertise, successes, and failures facilitates their development.

■ Planning Together

Rather than facing a seemingly impossible task of accommodating all of the special needs in your class alone, classroom teachers and special educators, working together, can generate plans that they are comfortable with and that are appropriate for the children in the class, building tools they will use over and over through the years.

Constructing an inclusion classroom is a long-term process, and teachers benefit greatly from the help and advice of special educators and other special education team members. When building our environment, it is important to work toward concrete, achievable goals. What do we expect to have in place in one year? Two years? It may take up to five years to achieve the inclusive classroom we want, after which we continually need to fine-tune it. As we work with the special education team and with diverse learners, and as we reflect on what works, what doesn't work, and what we would like to improve, we will become knowledgeable experts able to handle almost any situation.

Here's something to think about. While most teachers are committed to the teaching profession for the long term, many do not take a long term view and incorporate work done today for diverse learners or children with learning challenges into their classroom structure, believing (or hoping) the situation is unique to this year and not part of a long term plan. Taking the long view and making a multiyear plan consciously building a supportive structure recognizes the fact that there will always be children in our classes who need accommodations. It also adds value to the work we do and brings the satisfaction of building for the future. In addition, it helps us prioritize tasks so the work we spend the most time and effort on is the work that will have the biggest return in the long term. We need to use special educators and the rest of the special education team to help us build our inclusive structure.

■ Team Dynamics

A special education team is subject to many rules, procedural regulations, and reporting requirements, most of them determined by law. The school designates an official team leader, or liaison, who is responsible for communicating with the parents and the school and for ensuring that the paperwork is done correctly and within the prescribed time limits. However, there is always also a functional team leader, who may or may not be the same person as the official leader. The functional team leader's authority stems from an acknowledgement by the other team members that he knows the child best and understands the goals of the IEP and of inclusion.

Functional, or natural, leadership is as old as time. A group of hunter-gatherers sits around a campfire early in the morning, preparing to search for food. One person gets up and walks off to the east. No one follows. Another person rises and begins walking to the southwest. The rest of the people at the campfire follow. What happened? Was an election held to make this person the leader? No, but everyone is following him. Is this person the leader? Most definitely yes. Everyone follows him because they acknowledge that he is the most knowledgeable about and proficient at finding food.

If a classroom is geared toward general education, particularly if the teacher takes a hands-off approach to diverse learners, two things are likely to happen, namely, the functional team leader will probably be the special education teacher, and the classroom teacher will probably be unhappy with the services being provided.

When the classroom orientation is inclusion, when every student is part of every lesson, and when everyone's progress is important, the teacher becomes a coleader with the special educator; they understand what needs to be done, establish achievable goals, and work together to solve problems on behalf of the student. Obviously, this is the best scenario for all concerned, because both educators have the same agenda: to develop an environment and curricular goals that make it possible for diverse learners and children with learning disabilities to thrive in the classroom.

If either the classroom teacher or the special educator gives lip service to inclusion but really believes the child should be educated in a separate program, they will be working at cross purposes. As a result, both may feel overwhelmed. Each will essentially be working alone, thinking the other is not doing what she should, and the child will not get the services he is entitled to receive. If a team is not working together effectively, the first thing we need to do is articulate and discuss what inclusion means to each of the involved parties and come to an agreement everyone is comfortable with. Everyone on the team needs to be working toward the same goals with the same understanding.

■ Play a Leadership Role

No matter who the official team leader is, it is in the classroom teacher's best interests to take a leadership role. Children with IEPs, as well as those with diverse learning styles, spend the majority of their time in the regular education classroom, and their behavior and performance affect everything that goes on there. In reality, no matter what we do, it is not possible for the classroom teacher to remain uninvolved. For the team to be effective, our role is essential, because we have so much information on the way children with disabilities function and learn. Classroom teachers who leave it to the experts are often dissatisfied with the decisions they are responsible for carrying out. If teachers in an inclusive classroom can say, "I've tried that, and this is what happened," the team will be one step closer to developing the best possible plan for the success of the child. Teachers who have no accommodations in place are the ones who, year after year, child after child, find themselves with the difficult task of accommodating each individual and feel frustrated because no one seems to listen to (or follow) their suggestions.

When the classroom teacher views the child as a full member of the class and shares with the team how the child functions in the classroom, the special education teacher, the speech and language pathologist, the occupational therapist, and the school psychologist or guidance counselor can work together to devise practical, workable solutions and move the child forward. A team in which all the members work wholeheartedly with one another on behalf of the student achieves the best outcomes.

■ Use an Inclusive Lens

A special education team establishes goals for a child based on formal and informal test results, classroom observations, and suggestions and insights from the team members: the classroom teacher, specialists, and parents. A child whose needs are not adequately supported and/or who is frustrated by work that is too difficult will most likely exhibit behavior problems: not doing the work, acting out, making frequent trips to the restroom or the school nurse, disrupting classroom routines. Since misbehavior needs to be modified or redirected before learning can take place, the team may first need to concentrate on behavior goals and plans. It can be very difficult to change disruptive behavior in a general education classroom, because the child most likely developed them as a way to survive there in the first place. Teacher and child remain stuck in this struggle all year, the teacher becoming more and more frustrated and the child falling further and further behind. And even if the behavior plan does work to some extent, the child's basic skills, independence, and self-confidence as a learner are not being developed. This "learned helplessness" is frustrating for everyone.

Classroom teachers who have most of the common accommodations in place and who know their students and understand the curriculum can anticipate challenges, provide scaffolds, and modify the way they teach upcoming units of study, thus helping all students get more out of the material. Teachers who share their knowledge and understanding of their students and their challenges and who work with other team members to devise IEPs have more control. The team sees them as knowledgeable and able, and the adjustments and modifications put in place are more effective and tailored to their classroom and teaching styles.

An inclusive classroom environment enables a special education team to differentiate challenges posed by the environment from those stemming from a diverse learning or cognitive style or a learning disability. When most of the common accommodations have already been incorporated into the classroom, the causes of problems will be easier to determine, new accommodations will be easier to institute, and results will be more positive. Even in cases where we feel we are not receiving adequate special education support, an inclusive structure will support us and our students until we are able to get the help we need. If we are receiving good special education support, the inclusive structure enhances that support.

Over time, developing a reputation as a teacher who understands the needs of diverse learners will strengthen our ability to build the support we need and influence other members of the team. As we use inclusive practices and our success with all types of learners becomes evident, others will follow our lead, collaboration will become stronger, and the team will become more effective. Again, we cannot directly change another person, but by changing or making adjustments to what we do and to the environment around us, we can have a powerful influence on creating a more effective special education team.

We must also try to get the most out of the time a special educator *is* in our classroom. Small-group work, reteaching and/or extra practice activity stations, and the presentation of new material are more effective when there is an extra person in the room to help assess understanding and work with individual students who encounter difficulty. The special educator may also be able to provide assistive equipment, such as tape recorders, cassette players, books on tape, magnifiers for children with vision problems, word prediction software, and software that helps children organize their writing. They may also be able to provide or help you acquire computer programs that will allow the child to work independently or use different modalities to increase skills.

Teachers who use inclusive practices not only have more input into team decisions but also better understand the reasons for them. Committing ourselves to the idea that all children can succeed in a general education classroom and working in coleadership with the special educator makes us more effective and more supported teachers. Our feelings of being adrift in an untenable situation abate, and we are able to contribute valuable insights about the way learning-challenged children function in the classroom.

■ Know Where We're Going

Another important factor in building an effective special education team is making sure all team members are aware of the goals and what must be done to reach them. Learning-challenged children must be supplied with the accommodations listed on their IEP, and those responsible for day-to-day implementation must know what these accommodations are and how to carry them out. Many teachers may not know where to find the IEP or how to read it. The special education teacher needs to make sure that everyone on the team is aware of the child's challenges, the IEP goals, and the necessary accommodations. One way she can do this is by highlighting this information on the IEP. In an inclusion classroom the basic accommodations will automatically be provided, and adding new ones will not be difficult. (Accommodations may be more difficult additions in a general education classroom, but they are required by law.)

Classroom paraprofessionals are often overlooked when information regarding goals and accommodations is disseminated. In many cases they may be the ones who spend the most one-on-one time with a child, yet they may not have read the child's IEP and may be unaware of the academic goals and classroom accommodations listed there. Paraprofessionals are a valuable resource for helping children with disabilities progress. Guiding, training, supporting, and retaining them is an investment in the team and a way to increase the effectiveness of the classroom teacher and the special educator. When the paraprofessionals in the classroom are fully included and their input and ideas are valued, children make the best progress.

■ Weekly Meetings

An important mechanism that allows you to regularly share information and build the team is the weekly team meeting. This meeting can take several forms:

- You can meet alone with the special educator.
- You can meet with the special educator and other teachers who teach the same grade level.
- You can, if possible, meet with the special educator and others who provide services in your classroom.
- You can include paraprofessionals that work with children in your class.

The meetings should be focused on sharing relevant information, such as academics for the week ahead, behavioral challenges, or social issues impacting the success of the diverse learners in the classroom as well as any changes in students' home lives you are aware of that may require extra support. It's important to provide the team with information on any problems that occurred during the week, including missing or incomplete work or class assignments, class work that requires reteaching, and information on areas where you feel a child is in danger of falling behind, so you can work together to implement plans. It is also important that you receive information about what the special educator has been working on with the child and that you share information on the types of approaches that have proved successful or unsuccessful during the week, including any new accommodations that have been put in place, how they are working (or not), and if they need to be modified, changed, or discontinued. The value of these accommodations should be judged in terms of whether or not they enable the child to access the curriculum and be more independent.

You should also discuss the curriculum for the following week, focusing on areas that could be challenging for some of the students. You may want to discuss the makeup of small groups as well as those things the special educator may have to plan for or prepare in advance, including any needed scaffolding, curricular modifications, or alternative rubrics. All of these modifications should be evaluated and filed to be used in future years.

Upcoming long term projects and the types of supports that will be needed should be part of these discussions. If you are meeting with the special educator as a grade level group, and all classrooms at the grade level will be working on the same unit and project, discussing the curriculum is relevant to all. Maybe you can work out a schedule in which you come a bit early to talk about the specific children in your class with the special educator before the discussions surrounding curriculum begin. When the other grade level teachers join you, you can all meet to talk about the curriculum. You may then be able to leave while the special educator spends a bit of time with the other teacher discussing his students. However you set your meetings up, it is important to spend time sharing information and ideas about individual students as well as the curriculum. Between meetings, brief e-mails or conversations can be used to communicate with one another.

■ Rome Wasn't Built in a Day

Great teams develop over time. Team members must learn to help and support one another by sharing responsibility for the child. Collaboration that values the ideas of all members helps decrease turnover and makes the team more focused and functional.

If teamwork is key, where does that leave those who must work in a team with one or more members who are disinclined to work cooperatively for the benefit of children with diverse needs or, worse, are apathetic, hostile, or unwilling to share decision making? This is sometimes an unfortunate reality.

First, we can help ourselves by developing an inclusive classroom. In time, this will be the catalyst that gets the team moving in the right direction. Most of us are in our professions for the long haul. As we work year after year with our school's special educators, therapists, and guidance counselors, things will improve. By doing what we can to promote inclusive education, we will become natural leaders. We will be able to share our knowledge of the needs of the children in our classroom with the other team members, describe what does and doesn't work, and together create the best plan for each child. If we set an example by contributing all the background information we can, listening to the information provided by others, and viewing all suggestions with an open mind, others will follow our lead. We can take some of the following specific steps (see Goleman, 1998):

- Realize we cannot change someone else directly but that by changing our actions, we have a powerful affect on others.
- Understand that colleagues, like students, change step by step, and everyone needs encouragement along the way.
- Believe in a natural leadership that comes from doing our job well and interacting positively with others.
- Look at a problem from the perspective of all involved, and develop solutions that reflect each person's needs.
- Understand that teams are not formed just for this year; they are built and become better over the years.
- Listen to and consider all ideas. This does not mean members of the team cannot strongly disagree at times. It does mean we need to keep trying to understand one another's position and needs and continue to look for a solution that satisfies all parties.
- Provide information and training to paraprofessionals and others who need it, and then give them the autonomy to carry out their responsibilities.
- Make sure all team members are aware of the goals.
- Establish procedures for setting goals, monitoring progress toward them, and changing plans and methods if that progress doesn't materialize.

Effective special education teams take time and effort to build, but good teams support both the children in need and the adults charged with their education. The effort is eminently worthwhile.

In Summary

Be a leader by setting up an inclusive environment and knowing every child, and you will get better support from your special education team.

Develop the special education team for the long term—increase collaboration by trying to understand each person's perspective, and try to make plans that work for all team members.

Use the disability summaries in Chapter 2 to build common understanding.

Nurture and develop all members of the team, including paraprofessionals. Be supportive and collaborative.

Make sure all team members have access to information about IEP goals and accommodations.

At team meetings, share information about curriculum as well as academic, social, and behavioral issues of individual children.

Building an effective team takes time, but is well worth it.

Bibliography

ARMSTRONG, T. (1999). *Seven Kinds of Smart: Identifying and Developing Your Multiple Intelligences*. New York: New American Library.

ATWELL, N. (1998). *In the Middle: New Understanding About Writing, Reading and Learning*. New Hampshire: Heinemann.

BEANE, A. (2005). The Bully Free Classroom: Over 100 Tips and Strategies for Teachers K-8. Minneapolis: Free Spirit Publishing.

BIRSH, J.R. (2005). *Multisensory Teaching of Basic Language Skills*. 2nd edition. Baltimore: Brooks.

BURNS, M. (1992). *About Teaching Mathematics*: *A K-8 Resource*. New Hampshire: Heinemann.

CALKINS, L. (2006). *A Guide to the Writing Workshop*. New Hampshire: First Hand.

CLEMENTS, A. (1999). *The Landry News*. New York: Simon & Schuster Books for Young Readers.

DEUTSH SMITH, D. (2006). *Introduction to Special Education: Making* a *Difference,* 6th edition, *MyLabSchool Series*. Boston: Allyn & Bacon.

FLETCHER, R., AND PORTALUPI, J. (2001). *Writing Workshop*: *The Essential Guide from the Authors of Craft Lessons*. New Hampshire: Heinemann.

FOSNOT, C.T., AND DOLK, M. (2001). *Young Mathematicians at Work: Constructing Multiplication and Division*. New Hampshire: Heinemann.

FOUNTAS, I., AND PINNELL, G. (2001). *Guiding Readers and Writers: Teaching Comprehension Genre and Content Literacy*. New Hampshire: Heinemann.

FOUNTAS, I., AND PINNELL, G. (2006). *Reader's Notebook*. New Hampshire: Heinemann.

FOUNTAS, I., AND PINNELL, G. (2006–2008). *The Fountas and Pinnell Leveled Book List, K–8*. New Hampshire: Heinemann. Retrieved from *www.FountasandPinnellLeveledBooks.com*

GARDNER, H. (1999). *Intelligence Reframed: Multiple Intelligences for the 21st Century*. New York: Basic Books.

GLASSER, W. (1992). *The Quality School: Managing Students Without Coercion*. New York: Harper & Row.

GOLEMAN, D. (1998). *Working with Emotional Intelligence*. London: Bloomsbury Publishing Plc.

GRAY, C. (2000). *The New Social Story Book: Illustrated Edition*. Texas: Future Horizons, Inc.

HALLAHAN, D.P., AND KAUFFMAN, J.M. (2005) *Exceptional Learners: Introduction to Special Education*. 10th edition. Boston: Allyn & Bacon.

HIEBERT, J., CARPENTER, T. P., FENNEMA, E., FUSON, K. C., WEARNE, D., AND MURRAY, H. (1997). Making Sense: Teaching and Learning Mathematics with Understanding. Portsmouth, NH: Heinemann.

HELPGUIDE.org: A Trusted Non-Profit Resource. *www.helpguide.org/index.html*

HEWARD, W.L. (2005). *Exceptional Children: An Introduction to Special Education*. 7th edition. Englewood Cliffs, NJ: Merrill, an imprint of Prentice Hall.

KLUTH, P. (2003). *You're Going to Love This Kid: Teaching Students with Autism in the Inclusive Classroom*. Baltimore: Brooks.

KOHN, A. (1999). *Schools Our Children Deserve: Moving Beyond Traditional Classrooms and 'Tougher Standards.'* Boston: Houghton Mifflin.

QUILL, K. (2000). *Do, Watch, Listen, Say*. Baltimore: Brooks Publishing.

SchwabLearning.org: A parent's guide to Helping Kids with Learning Difficulties: *www.schwablearning.org*

SCHWARZ, P. (2006). *From Disability to Possibility: The Power of Inclusive Classrooms*. Portsmouth, NH: Heinemann.

TOURETTE'S DISORDER INFORMATION SUPPORT: *www.tourettes-disorder.com*

UNITED STATES DEPARTMENT OF HEALTH AND HUMAN SERVICES NATIONAL MENTAL HEALTH INFORMATION CENTER. *http://mentalhealth.samhsa.gov/publications/allpubs/SMA-3716/making.asp*

VAN DE WALLE, J. (2001). *Elementary and Middle School Mathematics Teaching Developmentally*. 4th edition. New York: Addison Wesley Longman, Inc.

VYGOTSKY, L.S. (1998). *The Collected Works of L.S. Vygotsky: Volume 3: Problems of the Theory and History of Psychology (Cognition and Language: A Series in Psycholinguistics)*. Edited by Robert W. Rieber and Jeffrey Wollock. New York: Springer.

ZEMELMAN, S., DANIELS, H., AND HYDE, A. (2005) *Best Practices: New Standards for Teaching and Learning*. 3rd edition. New Hampshire, Heinemann.

Index

accommodations
    common IEP accommodations, 41,
        41–44
    importance of (overview), 4–9, 11, 12
    inclusiveness and (overview), 4–9, 11,
        12
    independence and, 38, 40, 41, 42, 43–44
    as invisible, 74
    legal requirements on, 5, 53, 66
    long-term use of, 12, 42, 44, 46, 47, 118
    for math, 44–47
    for reading, 47–50
    for testing, 101–104
    for writing, 50–51
    See also specific disabilities
ADD
    ADHD vs., 17
    See also attention-deficit hyperactivity/
        disorder (ADD/ADHD)
ADHD
    ADD vs., 17
    Tourette's syndrome and, 36
    See also attention-deficit hyperactivity/
        disorder (ADD/ADHD)
arithmetical learning disability
    accommodations for, 34–35
    assignments for, 34
    definition, 33
    disability profile, 33–35
    views/descriptions of, 33–34

Asperger's autism (high-functioning
        autism)
    accommodations for, 25–26
    assignments for, 25
    definition, 24
    disability profile, 24–26
    helping with behavior, 95–96
    views/description of, 24–25
assessing students
    beginning of year, 56–57, 65, 99–
        100
    curriculum goals and, 56–57, 58, 65
    embedded assessments, 98, 101, 103
    end of year, 99, 100–101
    grading, 104–105
    middle of year, 99, 100
    retaking tests, 105–106
    rubrics, 99, 105
    self-assessments, 98
    standardized tests, 54, 57, 103
    summary, 107
    testing accommodations, 101–104
attention-deficit hyperactivity/disorder
        (ADD/ADHD)
    accommodations for, 19–20
    ADD vs. ADHD, 17
    assignments for, 18
    definition, 17
    disability profile, 17–20
    views/descriptions of, 17–18

behavior
    assumptions on, 86–87
    autistic children and, 95–96
    basic motivators of, 75–76
    chart on understanding, 83
    promoting positive behavior, 81, 82,
        84–86, 87–88, 97
behavior problems
    assumptions on, 86–87
    chart on understanding, 83
    home situation and, 85
    from learning challenges (summary list),
        92
    reading problems example, 93–95
    reasons for, 75–76, 81–84, 85, 86–88,
        92–95, 97
    rules/punishment approach, 81
    teacher's attitude/behavior and, 88–91
    team solutions, 120
    undocumented disabilities and, 92
belonging as basic need, 75
Berra, Yogi, 54
bodily/kinesthetic intelligence pathway,
    52
bullying, 74–75, 76, 88

child study group, 66
classroom
    areas of, 40–41
    as community, 74–76, 80
    displays, 38–39, 41
    focus accommodation and, 40
    layout, 39–41
    memory accommodation, 39
    organization accommodation, 39–40
    overview, 38–39
    preparation, 1–2
class selection, 2–3
Clements, Andrew, 69
communicating with parents
    collaboration and, 109–110
    home-school plans, 110
    listening to parents, 110, 111, 112–113
    overview, 108–109
    progress reporting, 112–113
    reaching out/understanding, 110–112

summary, 114
    when parents are upset, 112–113
Creating the Peaceable School program, 75
curriculum
    grouping students to learn, 57
    as inclusive, 59–64
    as multilevel, 59
    workshops and, 59–64

desk/table arrangements, 41, 44
direction giving, 6–7, 17, 19, 25, 26, 28,
    41, 43, 67
disability profiles
    accommodations and, 15–16
    arithmetical learning disability, 33–35
    Asperger's autism (high-functioning
        autism), 24–26
    attention-deficit hyperactivity/disorder
        (ADD/ADHD), 17–20
    description, 14–16
    dysgraphia, 30–32
    dyslexia, 27–29
    nonverbal learning disabilities
        (NVLD), 21–23
    role/use of, 11, 14–16, 92, 111–112,
        117
    Tourette's syndrome, 36–37
distraction limiting, 19, 41, 44
dysgraphia
    accommodations for, 31–32
    assignments for, 31
    definition, 30
    disability profile, 30–32
    views/descriptions of, 30–31
dyslexia
    accommodations for, 28–29
    assignments for, 28
    definition, 27
    disability profile, 27–29
    views/descriptions of, 27–28

expectations
    accepting differences and, 70–72
    beneficial expectations, 70
    harmful effects of, 70–72
    high expectations, 70–72

Fountas, Irene, 50
Fountas and Pinnell Leveled Book List, The (Fountas and Pinnell), 50
Fountas and Pinnell Reader's Notebook (Fountas and Pinnell), 48
freedom as basic need, 75
friendship promotion
    class meetings and, 76–78
    overview, 76–79, 80
    student quiz on, 76–77
    website for, 78
fun as basic need, 75

Gardner, Howard, 51–52
Glasser, William, 75, 76
grading, 104–105
Gray, Carol, 15, 26

handouts use, 11, 42
homework recommendations, 5, 19, 58, 59, 67, 85, 110, 112
hyperlexia, 21

IEP requirements/accommodations
    common accommodations, 41, 41–44
    evaluating, 66
    legal requirements on, 5, 53, 66
    for math, 44–47
    for reading, 47–50
    for writing, 50–51
intelligence pathways, 51–52
interpersonal intelligence pathway, 52
intrapersonal intelligence pathway, 52

labeling children, 66
Laundry News, The (Clements), 68–69
learning styles, 51–52, 53
lesson format, 7
library in classroom, 31, 49
logical/mathematical intelligence pathway, 52
long-term memory, 39, 45

math
    accommodations/IEPs for, 44–47
    assessing skills, 99–100, 101

classroom postings for, 45, 46, 47
    workshop goals/supports, 63–64
mini-lessons
    use of, 7–8, 29, 51, 58–59, 63, 103
    work following, 6
musical intelligence pathway, 52

needs, basic
    overview, 75
    unmet power need/effects, 75–76
nonverbal learning disabilities (NVLD)
    accommodations for, 23
    assignments for, 22–23
    definition, 21
    disability profile, 21–23
    views/description of, 21–22

overheads use, 23, 42

paraprofessionals, 16, 73, 116, 122, 124, 125
parents
    on education teams, 116
    See also communicating with parents; teams
Pinnell, Gay Su, 50
power as basic need
    description, 75
    meeting/effects, 76
    unmet/effects, 75–76

Quill, Kathleen, 15

reading
    accommodations/IEPS for, 47–50
    assessing skills, 99, 100, 101
    behavior problem example, 93–95
    "bookmark" for, 49
    at child's level, 47–50, 94–95
    prereading strategy checklist, 49
    workshop goals/supports, 60–61
routines (overview)
    benefits of, 68
    modifying, 68
rules of classroom
    establishing, 75, 76
    posting, 75

special educators
  taking child from classroom, 115, 116
  See also teams
Stand and Deliver, 70
standardized tests, 54, 57, 103

teaching
  cheerleading/effects, 70–71
  curiosity of teachers, 64
  developing individual style, 68–70
  knitting analogy, 54–56
  qualities of great teachers, 3–4, 64, 90–91
  self-assessment for inclusiveness, 72–74
  success at, 3–4, 68–70, 90–91
teams
  behavior problems and, 120
  collaboration with, 9–10, 117
  communicating, 116, 117, 122–123
  core members, 116
  goals and, 117–118, 119, 120, 121–122
  IEPs and, 115, 116, 117, 118, 119, 120, 121–122, 125
  improving, 115, 123–124
  inclusiveness and, 117–118, 119–121, 124
  leadership, 118–120
  meetings, 122–123
  summary, 125
teasing, 74–75, 76, 88
text-to-speech word processing feature, 31, 43

Tourette's syndrome
  accommodations for, 37
  definition, 36
  disability profile, 36–37
  views/descriptions of, 36–37

United States Department of Health and Human Services, 78

verbal/linguistic intelligence pathway, 52
visual/spatial intelligence pathway, 52
Vygotsky, L. S., 58

websites
  on ADD, 17
  book titles by reading level, 50
  friendship promotion, 78
  teacher's personal site, 59
word banks/walls, 42, 43, 49, 51
working memory, 39, 45
workshops
  for math, 63–64
  overview, 59–60, 65
  for reading, 60–61
  for writing, 61–63
writing
  accommodations/IEPs for, 50–51
  assessing skills, 99, 100, 101
  process progress chart, 62
  workshop goals/supports, 61–63

zone of proximal development (ZPD), 58